Ibiza

inspired images from the island of dance

Edited by Ben Turner

EBURY
PRESS

ABOUT THE AUTHOR: Ben Turner is editor and co-founder of *MUZIK* — the ultimate dance music magazine. He began his career at IPC's *Melody Maker*, where he edited the Orbit dance pages before launching *MUZIK* in May 1995. He was also *The Guardian*'s dance writer in 1994. In 1998 he spent one year as A&R Manager at Deconstruction/BMG, where he signed The Dreem Teem and Norman Cook's Freak Power project. He's managed to fit in 15 visits to Ibiza during this short time. At 25, he's the youngest ever editor of an IPC title.

SPECIAL THANKS to the contributors Colin Butts, Andy Crysell, Rob Da Bank, Dave Fowler, Andy Pemberton and Frank Tope; and the photographers Adrian Batty, Jamie Baker, Hamish Brown, Grant Fleming, Vincent McDonald, Leelu Morris, Daniel Newman, Ronnie Randall and Rip. Thanks also to Jake Lingwood at Ebury Press and Rachel Pearce at IPC.

MUZIK is published on the second Wednesday of every month by IPC Magazines Limited, King's Reach Tower, Stamford Street, London SE1 9LS. For subscription enquiries call: 01444 445555 (fax no: 01444 445599) or write to: Quadrant Subscription Services, FREEPOST CY1061, Haywards Heath, West Sussex RH16 3ZA.

PHOTOGRAPHIC CREDITS:

Adrian Batty: pages 13 left, 17 top, 20 left, 23 left, 24 bottom left, 31 (both), 38 bottom, 44, 52 bottom, 57, 59 bottom, 78, 98, 103 left, 118, 119 left, 125, 129, 134 top, 136-137, 143

Jamie Baker: 8 top right, 12 both, 14-15, 18-19, 29 top, 34 left, 36, 39 (both), 42 right, 49 right, 52 top, 53, 54, 60 (all), 61 (all), 62 right, 63 top left, 63 right, 64 (both), 65 (both), 66-67 bottom, 68 bottom, 69 right,70 left, 71 (both), 72 right, 76, 77, 80-83 (all), 90 (both), 92 bottom, 94 middle left, 96-97, 99, 108-109 bottom, 109 right, 114 left, 115, 116, 117 left, 120-123 (all), 128, 131 top, 132-133 (all), 135 left

Vincent Macdonald: pages 2-3

Leelu Morris: pages 9 left, 39 right, 40 top, 41 (all), 47, 87, 88, 89, 110 bottom, 126

Daniel Newman: pages 4, 13 right, 24 top, 25 top, 32, 34-35, 37, 46 left, 49 left, 50-51, 55, 58, 69 left, 70 right, 74-75, 79, 85, 86 bottom, 112 left, 114 right, 124, 127 right, 130, 134 bottom, 138 top, 139, 140-141 (both)

Ronnie Randall: pages 6-7, 20-21, 23 bottom right, 30, 33, 42 left, 48, 62 left, 66 left, 67 top & bottom right, 68 top, 94 bottom left, 95 (both), 102, 103 right, 104 bottom, 106-107, 138 bottom, 142 bottom

Rip: pages 16, 17 bottom, 19 right, 45, 56, 91 top, 92 top, 94 top left, 131 bottom, 142 top

Dave Swindells: pages 26-27

Designed by Dan Newman

Printed and bound in Singapore by Tien Wah Press

First published in Great Britain in 1999

10 9 8 7 6 5 4 3 2 1

© IPC Magazines Ltd.,1999

Foreword © Danny Rampling, 1999

Ebury Press
Random House, 20 Vauxhall Bridge Road, London SW1V 2SA

Random House Australia Pty Limited
20 Alfred Street, Milsons Point, Sydney, New South Wales 2061, Australia

Random House New Zealand Limited
18 Poland Road, Glenfield, Auckland 10, New Zealand

Random House South Africa (Pty) Limited
Endulini, 5A Jubilee Road, Parktown 2193, South Africa

Random House UK Limited Reg. No. 954009

A CIP catalogue record for this book is available from the British Library

ISBN 0-09-186934-X

Papers used by Ebury Press are natural, recyclable products made from wood grown in sustainable forests

DJ Danny Tenaglia outside Mambo and Cafe Del Mar © Vincent McDonald

Amnesia 1990

Contents

6   **Ibiza changed my life** by Danny Rampling

10   **Introduction** by Ben Turner

14   **Ibiza – my love affair** by Colin Butts

26   **Ibiza – the discovery** by Andy Crysell

50   **Ibiza – the British invasion** by Andy Pemberton

74   **Ibiza – the music** by Frank Tope

96   **Ibiza – the decadence** by Dave Fowler

120   **Ibiza – the rebirth** by Rob Da Bank

Ibiza
changed my life

By Danny Rampling

I FIRST WENT TO IBIZA WITH A FRIEND IN 1980 WHEN I WAS 18. WE WENT ON A TWENTIES holiday in May, so it was slightly out of season. We didn't quite know what Twenties was at the time, but they had such cheap tickets we couldn't refuse. This was my first holiday away on my own, so you can imagine the apprehension and the excitement about not knowing what to expect. We arrived at nighttime and the first thing I became aware of was the scent of the island. Ibiza has a special scent with the pine trees and fresh air, with the airport being so close to the ocean. It's a magical smell to arrive to, and it gets me every time. We were young boys out for a good time and we were unaware of the Ku club. But we could tell Ibiza was a vibrant island. We did visit Ibiza Town and I was taken back by this beautiful ancient town. That first holiday had me hooked on Ibiza.

I went back later that same summer with the same friends again. And then the next summer. And then it was the summer after that when I met Nicky Holloway for the very first time. I was aware of him as a DJ and we soon forged a friendship. I went to his events and soon ended up working with him. It was a few years before we discovered the truly amazing side to the nightlife. We were still clubbing in clubs like Es Paradis but most guys weren't really into dancing. It wasn't the done thing, but we loved it. It also meant we had far more chance of meeting girls because we seemed to be more fun. And yes, we did meet lots of girls. They were queuing up!

I went to work and live in America for a year, and so it was some time before I went back to Ibiza. By this time, Nicky was running his Special Branch parties out there and these

San Antonio beach

West End, San Antonio

were a great alternative to the regular club scene in Ibiza. By now we were aware of Amnesia but we were restricted by money because these clubs were out of our price range. It cost £15 in those days, and people do forget how expensive it is for young people today.

I read an article in *The Face* about Amnesia, the club which never sleeps, and I was determined to check it out. When I did, everything I had read was true. I was captivated by the atmosphere. I'd never seen anything like it. I danced my ass off in front of the speakers. Coming from a funky soul scene into this supercharged tribal energy was incredible. I immediately noticed how positive and colourful the crowd was, and people were sharing their good times, obviously with the help of MDMA. Oakey disappeared to the DJ booth for most of the night, Nicky went to the bar and I just danced and forged friendships with a few English travellers I spotted in the crowd. I was so impressed by the communication in this open-air club. At 6 am the night ended with the sun coming up just as Alfredo played Cyndi Lauper. We didn't want that night to end. We did get to sleep, but it took some time. As soon as we woke up, we went straight back to Amnesia, and did the same every night for the rest of our stay. We'd found the holy grail.

My experiences inspired me to go home and give it my best shot at creating a version of Amnesia in London, which we did in a very different way. Obviously we didn't have an open-air club at Shoom, but we managed to create a similar volume of energy. I realise now that Amnesia was really a continuation of the Studio 54 and Paradise Garage legacy. It

Atlantis

was the European equivalent with many of the same people who frequented those clubs in New York.

Ibiza has a magnetic energy which attracts so many different people, but they all seem to have a connecting spirit in that they're looking for fun. It really is the clubbing mecca of the world. But it's also the tranquility of the island, the landscapes and the people who are so welcoming which makes Ibiza so special.

Ibiza has been wonderful to me. Hearing Alfredo gave me the inspiration to go forward, and the music I've played in clubs for the last ten years is built around my passion and experiences from Ibiza. In more recent times, I do go to Ibiza as much to have a peaceful time as to club. I've had loads of crazy times there and, at this point in my life, the peaceful times tend to outweigh the mad ones.

There is a lot of mystery surrounding Ibiza but one always has to remember that there are a lot of people on the island with very broad imaginations! Thailand and America are also close to my heart, but Ibiza's nightlife has more to offer than any European destination. I don't think my love affair will ever end with Ibiza. I have made so many good friends on the island, who I look forward to seeing every year, and clubs likle Pacha and El Divino affect me every time I walk into them because they reflect the true spirit of Ibiza. I still enjoy their intimacy. Ibiza, to me, is simply a creative source, a friend, a lover and a home.

Ibiza
inspired images from the island of dance

By Ben Turner

THIS BOOK IS, AS NIGHTCLUB OWNER BRAZILIO FAMOUSLY SAID ABOUT HIS STUNNING Ku club, 'the mirror of Ibiza'. It's a collection of images and words which show the contrast and contradiction of the most infectious party island in the world. In an attempt to reflect the vivid images and insane experiences which everyone associated with dance culture has experienced at some stage in their lives, I decided that like all the other beautiful cities and towns all over the world, Ibiza deserved to have a book of pictures dedicated to the holiday experience which today attracts around one million tourists each year. If this book feels remarkably fresh to you, then that's probably because the last thing on your mind on a chaotic two-week sojourn here is trying to capture that classic photograph of you on the dancefloor at Space on a Sunday afternoon.

As editor of club culture bible *Muzik* magazine, it's our duty to worry about such matters. So over the last four summers in which *Muzik* has existed, we've collected thousands of images from Ibiza. With the help of other photographers from our scene, we've put together a selection of the most inspired, the most evocative and, in places, the most provocative of pictures which best sum up the island's vast extremes. From the beauty of Ibiza Town and the infamous rock at Atlantis, to the lager lords falling over in San Antonio town, the book reflects how the island comfortably accommodates the rich next to the poor. Combining club photography from Pacha, Ku and Amnesia to the beach parties and events on the hills, to amazing hotels and sunsets right through to the characters and hippies who

Pacha

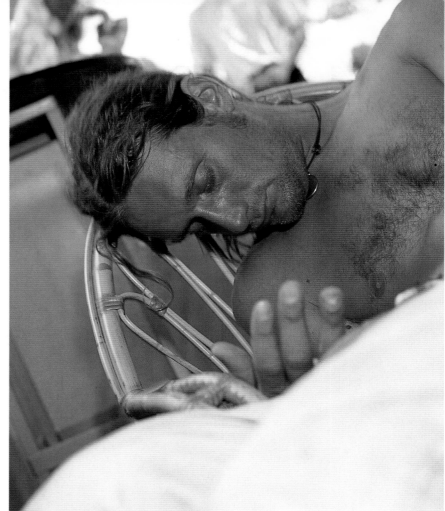

inhabit the island, you can see all sides of the Great White Island.

Ibiza is described by many as being a magical island. It's on a fault line and rumoured to be on a bedrock of quartz, which is what generates the special energy and vibe which has attracted so many people to settle here. It's what gives the island its true spiritual feel, and is perhaps the perfect explanation for what makes this place special. So many British tourists arrive here for a fortnight and fail to see half of what goes on in this tiny island, and this book is an attempt to try and educate but, essentially, stimulate. With six essays written on the different historic aspects of Ibiza, **Inspired Images** guides you through its history, the great British club invasion, the musical changes on the island, right through to the rebirth of Ibiza club culture over the past three years.

I first visited Ibiza in the summer of 1994 as a true clubber on a two-week holiday. As a sheltered boy from Oxford, I experienced then so little of what I have now seen after fifteen visits to the island. And I'm still discovering so much more about the place. The

Ben Turner & Liverpool Phil. Amnesia, 7am

Renaissance at Pacha

reality is, that once locked into the grip of the island's club scene, it's hard to take time out and see the beauty of Formentera and spend time unwinding on the north of the island. The tempo of the island is so addictive, that you have to discipline yourself to experience the charm of its other side. In Ibiza the best-laid plans disappear within hours and the temptation to indulge in all its riches becomes too much. Spiritually, Ibiza can literally move mountains, as The Shamen's anthem from 1990, 'Progen' stated. It's a place of incredible extremes of pleasure and pain, where the highs can hurt as much as the hardest of lows. It's a place which has filled me with passion forever.

Ibiza – Inspired Images frm the Island Of Dance is aimed at anybody who has partied on the island in the last ten years. It has truly changed so many people's lives, as the experiences from clubbers, DJs, journalists, locals and club promoters printed here clearly convey. With Ibiza, as clubland character Eirik the Viking states later in this book, if you treat it well, it will treat you well back. And that's the main reason why this book has been made. Enjoy.

chapter one

Ibiza my love affair

By Colin Butts

DANNY RAMPLING ONCE SAID, 'ANYONE WHO HAS SPENT ANY LENGTH OF TIME ON THE island of Ibiza nearly always feels as though a piece of it belongs to them – or maybe a piece of them to Ibiza.' The only problem with magic is that whilst it can keep you forever enthralled, as soon as you are shown how it's done, the spellbinding captivity in which it once held you is lost forever.

And for me, during my second visit last summer, the magic was indeed lost. It heralded the end of a 12-year love affair. Like the end of any love affair, I've a mixture of emotions: sadness, regret, anger...they are all there.

To understand why a relationship is in trouble, one needs to understand a little of its history, particularly how it started. My relationship with Ibiza began in earnest when I had the misfortune to rep for Twenties holidays at the end of 1986. In 1987 I was back again, suffering the Union Jack shorts and enless renditions of 'Ere We Go'. Eventually it got too much, so I hung up my badge and the end of the season was spent taking group photographs on the official Ibiza Beach Party and working as a bouncer at The Star Club (now called Kaos).

At that time, Cafe Del Mar (owned by Ramon Guival and Carlos Andrea) was the domain of a few in the know, backgammon-playing locals and workers, while ex-holiday reps made up most of the DJs. The Milk Bar was a burger joint called Colonel Duff's and Ku (now Privilege) was a place to go for an expensive meal and to hang out with 1980s pop stars.

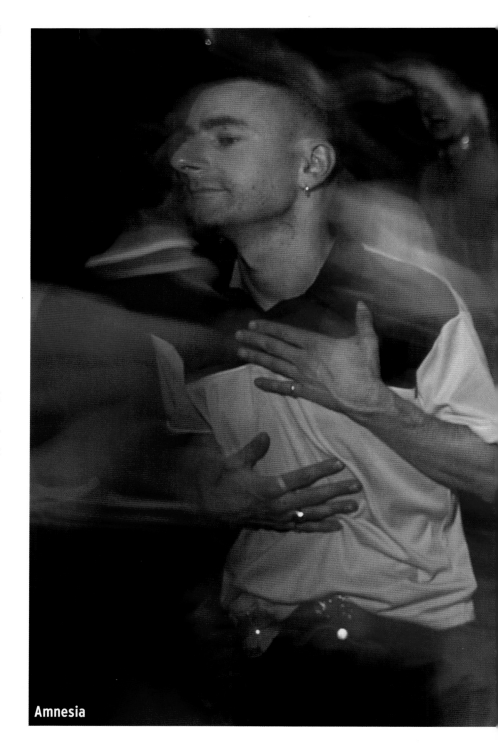

Amnesia

Cafe Del Mar owner Ramon Guival

In retrospect, I would love to be able to claim all sorts of affiliation to the birth of the scene; of getting down to Alfredo at Amnesia, appreciating the Bedouin type ambience of the Project Bar, and playing backgammon with Sid and Barnesly John at Cafe Del Mar. The truth of it was that although I went to the closing of Amnesia in 1987, I got the day wrong and turned up on my moped in the middle of a thunderstorm on the night after the closing. Yes, we used to hang out at the Project Bar, but in truth, it was more the appeal of the Geordie girls outside rather than the embryonic acid house goings-on inside that attracted us. And yes, I did play Sid at backgammon down the Del Mar, but the cheating scouse bastard kept fleecing me, so even that was but a brief association.

What we did notice however, was that the tassley boots and stone-washed denim that ruled Ibiza Town began to give way to baggy shirts, luminous colours and dungarees as the 1987 season drew to a close. Something was going on, but it was something that the majority of us were in truth, pretty much unaware of. Still, whatever it was, we all wanted more of it.

During the following winter I bought myself an old Triumph Herald, then in April 1988 I crammed a small home recording studio and Atari computer into it, and took a leisurely drive to Ibiza for the start of the season. The plan was to do a bit of songwriting, write a book and just generally chill out and have a good time. Somehow though, it all went wrong and I got roped into running a venue called the Bronco Bar-B-Q (which is now where they hold Sundance). My nightly duties were basically to compere the evening and take the piss out of as many people as possible (that bit was fun), then to play/sing 'Show Me The Way To Go Home', and busk along to out-of-tune reps before taking my clothes off every night in front of 400-plus pissed holidaymakers. The festivities ended with me spending an hour playing a few records and trying to squeeze S'Express or Rob Base & DJ E-Z Rock in between 'Shout' and 'Come On Eileen', finally rounding things off with Climie Fisher's seminal 'Rise To The Occasion'. As the record crackled to a finish on wholly unappreciative ears, the distant sound of fading football songs and faint stench of puke made us stick two fingers up and say good riddance to the lot of them, as we put our feet up and had a spliff before heading into town.

Meanwhile, something strange was going on. Whilst we were down The Star Club listening to The Beastie Boys, hordes of mopeds, buzzing like bronchial mosquitoes, were making their way towards San Rafael and Amnesia. Two good friends of mine who owned The Charleston spent the beginning of the season pouring over a music mag with furrowed brows, wondering how and why it was claimed that they were the bar in San Antonio. The reason was that a ginger-haired lad with a Rod Stewart haircut, who used to make a bit of a nuisance of himself when we'd go for beach BBQ's (Tony Wilson), and an oriental looking 'tassely boot boy' (Trevor Fung) simply played their mix tapes in the bar, and that was all that was needed to ensure its popularity. The pink and grey garage-sized bar was suddenly overrun with people whose crowning glory was no longer

back-combed, and in the resulting confusion my unpaid bar bill got bigger and bigger – long live acid house!

What might seem strange now is that San Antonio was still a place where many of the workers, scallies and wannabes used to congregate. Somewhere which rarely gets a mention yet was a regular meeting place of many of the main movers and shakers was a small bar called The Madhouse, now a small pizza restaurant called Amore Mio. Promoters and DJs were always dropping in for a drink, but despite the owner's attempts to stop it, the area around the bar was the one where most of those who understood what was going on would make their money. At the time it wasn't just drugs which provided a means of income but 'kiting', a far easier pursuit then than now, with no credit card terminals to 'spoil' things.

The Madhouse changed its name to Legends and for the wrong reason that is exactly what it ended up becoming. At the end of the season (which then lasted from May until November instead of July to September) there were a lot of problems with Moroccans, who were allegedly attacking tourists, sometimes at knifepoint. On 1 November 1988 a young Moroccan came into the virtually empty bar shouting and hollering. There were less than a dozen people in there, mainly bouncers and bar owners, so little attention was paid to him. However, a few hours (and several Jaegermeisters) later, he came back up the hill shouting and screaming with what looked like a little posse with him. It turned

The Egg at San Antonio

out he was on his own, but not knowing this, two off-duty bouncers chased him around the corner armed with a fruit knife and a baseball bat. What happened next remains unclear, but the upshot of it was one very dead Moroccan and two 14-year jail sentences. The postscript to this tragic story for me highlights both what I used to feel was the charm and the frustration of Ibiza. One of the two Brits went on the run and was for a time the most wanted man in the Balearics. Through the grapevine he heard that the bar owner (who was also a friend) was going to be held responsible for the murder, which apart from anything else, would have resulted in the him losing his family. Despite having an escape route planned, the fugitive rang the police station to give himself up.

'Sorry,' said the voice on the other end of the phone. 'No officers are here who speak English – can you stay where you are and ring back tomorrow?'

It was whilst sitting in The Madhouse during the season that we started to read or hear about workers from the preceding summer, workers who we'd previously assumed to be just scallies like 90 per cent of the rest of us. They were starting up 'raves' and there were pictures of massive queues of people outside newly opened London clubs with headlines screaming about a new movement. There were also tales of penthouse flats in Covent Garden and wads of cash. We sort of recognised them to nod at or by Christian name: 'Isn't that Nicky, the guy with the big nose who used to lead round groups of tourists?' Or, 'Ian. He's the Asian bloke who's brother Guy works for Thomsons.' And, 'Danny

1987 the Ibiza anthems

1 PROMISED LAND Joe Smooth (DJ International)
2 NUDE PHOTO Rhythim Is Rhythim (Transmat)
3 ACID THUNDER Fast Eddie (DJ International)
4 JOIN THE CHANT Nitzer Ebb (Mute)
5 THE WHOLE OF THE MOON The Waterboys (Chrysalis)
6 CAN U DANCE Fast Eddie (DJ International)
7 JIBARO Elkin & Nelson (CBS)
8 STONEFOX CHASE Area Code 618 (Polydor)
9 YE KE YE KE Mory Kante (Barclay)
10 BABY WANTS TO RIDE Jamie Principle

compiled by Pippi – Pacha resident

Es Cavallet nudist beach

or something, said he was a DJ and used to be down The Project Bar all the time...'

What the fuck was going on? Slowly, it began to dawn on us as we became aware of an inexorable change taking place in our little world. Then one night, we were presented with these little capsules, and the rest, as they say...

I won't bore you with my own personal Ecstasy history. Suffice to say that eventually a whole new world of Black & White parties, dancing through sunrise and gurning in the most beautiful clubs in the world suddenly opened up to me. The intervening years saw my own musical tastes and attitude to clubbing mature and refine, along with most other people's.

And therein lies the problem. Nowadays, if someone says 'Hello' to me at a urinal, I'm more likely to say 'Fuck off' than 'How many you had?' I'm all for live and let live, for youngsters to make their own narcotic journey of discovery, but selfish though it may seem, I'd rather they did so not at the expense of my enjoyment. I'm not a DJ, these aren't my fans, so I don't have to be nice to them if they irritate me.

Moreover, if it was just pilled-up, happy 18-year-olds that were invading the clubs in Ibiza, it probably wouldn't be so bad. Unfortunately, what is now happening in Ibiza is that the line between the two distinct yet often confused (by the media at least) cultures of San An lager lout and paid-up clubber, are becoming increasingly nebulous.

One of the reasons Danny Rampling gives for his recent embracing of more garage-influenced records is that the audiences which enjoy this type of music tend to consist of a higher ratio of females, and girls make the atmosphere in a club much warmer. One of the main complaints in Ibiza in 1998 was that the ratio in many clubs was 70-80 per cent male. Not only this, but the predominant type of male on display in clubs like Manumission and A Clockwork Orange, were the ones attracted by the salacious *Ibiza Uncovered* series (is it just a coincidence that the two clubs featured in this series were Manumission and Clockwork?).

Rampling said that it was probably the best time he'd had out there for half a decade. Well, with the possible exception of Bora Bora, for me the opposite was true. Mainly for reasons of research and economy, I was based near San An, which I had to visit occasionally because some friends still work there. Walking round the West End and the increasingly commercialised stretch around Cafe Del Mar, I soon had my fill of what's best described as 'Ibiza Uncovered' devotees. The problem was that the same kind of person also started turning up in most of the clubs. Even many of the workers now adopt a wholly unjustified savoir faire just because they haven't utilised the return part of their flight ticket, which when questioned, normally turns out to be a savoir rien.

The DJs and promoters are cosseted from what is fast becoming for many the real Ibiza. It's an Ibiza of hustling flying teams, endless queuing for taxis, huge sums of money to get into clubs and even vaster sums of money for drinks. Apart from the inside of clubs and San Antonio, many see little else of the island. They're led to believe that they daren't miss

Pacha

a single night out, which leaves little time to visit beaches like Beniras or some of the other glorious places on the island.

Like many of the DJs, I've often been cosily ensconced in a nice villa surrounded by friends. I've a car over there and don't pay to get into clubs; I blag drinks and even a few meals; I'm friends with most of the dealers, so if I choose a poison it's not normally a financial consideration, yet despite this and a general reluctance to put my hand in my pocket, in a week I still managed to spend over £600. God only knows what the average up-for-it holiday maker is spending.

I've always said that those who write Ibiza off every year are just sad old gits passed their sell-by date. New converts to the island will get different things out of it, so maybe my parting with Ibiza is like the end of a love affair after all. Ibiza feeds off the vitality of youth and perhaps shouldn't be shackled by the demands of an ageing lover, desperate not to see the partner he has shared so many unique experiences with casually toss him aside to find solace in a younger model. It's sad and painful imagining an ex enjoying anything with someone else, things you once enjoyed together; there is something sad and painful about an ex continuing to enjoy herself in spite of you.

During its history Ibiza has been invaded by Byzantines, Saracens, Vandals and Normans – most of its grandest statues pay testimony to heroes who thwarted the pirate invasions

Sa Trincha

Pacha

Space

Carl Cox, LTJ Bukem & Andy Carroll at Ibiza airport

of the 15th and 16th centuries. Yet the most successful invaders, the ones who have changed the economy and very psyche of the island, have done so without even having to draw a sword. They have drawn riches from the island which would surpass the wildest dreams of their pirate predecessors, yet their ammunition can be clearly seen juddering around the baggage carousel every day during the summer, in aluminium record boxes.

As a result of all of this, the temporada (what the locals call the season) is becoming ever shorter, which means prices must become ever dearer. These are the New Pirates.

You don't need to be Einstein to work out that I'm indeed becoming a sad old git, nor be Nostradamus to predict that I'll be out there this summer larging it with everyone else. However, British club promoters should take note that if Ibiza carries on down the blatantly commercial and spiritualless path that it's on, then it will have to undergo the greatest metamorphosis in its history to regain the magic with which it has been so long associated.

See you at Space.

Colin Butts is author of *Is Harry on the Boat?*

Cream at Amnesia

1988 the Ibiza anthems

1 LET ME LOVE YOU FOR TONIGHT Karyiya (Sleeping Bag)
2 VOODOO RAY   A Guy Called Gerald (Rham)
3 I'LL HOUSE YOU Jungle Brothers (Gee Street)
4 CARINO T Coy (Deconstruction)
5 ELECTRA Jibaro (ffrr)
6 CAN YOU PARTY Royal House (Gee Street)
7 A SPLIT SECOND Rigormortis (Antler Subway)
8 BREAK FOR LOVE Raze (Columbia)
9 DEVOTION Inner City (Elektra)
10 BAMBOLERO Gypsy Kings (Sony)

compiled by Pippi – Pacha resident

Playa D'en Bossa Beach

chapter two

Ibiza
the
discovery

By Andy Crysell

Club legend Max reading that historic Sun front cover story

BLINKING IN THE BRIGHT MEDITERRANEAN LIGHT, THEY LOOKED MUCH LIKE ALL THE OTHER lads stepping off that flight from Gatwick in September of 1987. Armed with duty-free cigarettes, ludicrously vivid shorts and a wad of pesetas, they doubtless guessed their week-long holiday on Ibiza would be a laugh. Yet they can't have imagined the endless nights of inconceivable fun this jaunt would eventually bestow on thousands of others.

These lads were Paul Oakenfold, Danny Rampling, Nicky Holloway and Johnny Walker, and they were to go home with more than just dubious tales of sexual conquest, chronic sunburn and a roll of photographs which seemed like a good idea at the time. In a matter of months, they would change the face of the UK's club scene, its youth culture and indeed the very sound of pop music forever. It was going to be quite a holiday...

The specific details of this momentous story run thus: they were invited to Ibiza by south London-based cousins Trevor Fung and Ian St Paul. A DJ and club promoter respectively, they'd been visiting the island since 1980, firstly as regular package-holiday tourists, then travelling outside of the cheap and cheerful confines of San Antonio to discover a world of palatial clubs and strange, beautiful people. Fung had DJed at various venues on the island, including a short stint at Amnesia. Then, at the beginning of the 1987 season, he and St Paul opened a bar in San Antonio called The Project – a name Fung also used for a club he ran in Streatham, south London, with Paul Oakenfold. It's fair to say they were truly smitten with life on Ibiza and now they were keen to share it with their mates.

So into this magical world came our unsuspecting foursome, on a crash course with an epiphany. Prior to their imminent baptism in this new scene, Paul Oakenfold was a hip-hop DJ, Rampling an up-and-coming soul DJ, Johnny Walker a respected funk spinner and Nicky Holloway the man behind Special Branch, a popular fixture of London nightlife in the 1980s.

All of which meant they came to the island with firm ideas of what clubbing was about. It was about dressing seriously, sticking to one style of music and being unflinchingly cool. Or, as Fung, who'd long felt dismay for the state of things back in London, puts it, 'It was about playing to a crowd who refused to listen to lively music, always dressed in boring black and always gave off a bad attitude.'

It was on their second night in Ibiza that they first tasted both Ecstasy and the island's more spirited approach to clubbing. Johnny Walker, now boss of the Cheeky and Champion labels, takes up the story.

'Trevor knew all about the E. He said it was amazing, that we should try some. So we took our pills at about midnight, in a San Antonio club called Nitelife, where this Spanish DJ called Carlos was playing really early Chicago house on the Trax label.

'When we came up on the E we didn't know what the hell was going on — only that we felt fantastic, everything looked sparkly and colourful, and we were up for a great night out. At about three in the morning we all bundled into a taxi and went to Amnesia. We walked inside, heard the music, saw the people, and that was it...'

Situated on the road between San Antonio and Ibiza Town, Amnesia looks no more spectacular than any other white-walled Spanish building from the outside. It could easily be just another of the many places selling local pottery along this stretch of Tarmac. Step inside, however, and it's like you're gliding through an opulent temple. Better still, back then it was an alfresco temple, open to the countless stars above, with resident DJ Alfredo playing an astonishing mix of music to almost as many stars on the dancefloor. Actors, models and pop dignitaries like Mick Jagger and George Michael would come up to shake the hand of this Argentinian at the end of each night. Amid the celebrities were fashionable Italians and French, wayward members of European aristocracy, seasoned beatniks and Ibiza's most eccentric residents – a Technicolor mix of transvestites, poets, painters and professional extroverts.

There were very few British, however, and many agree it was the happy coincidence of these fresh-faced newcomers and the increasing availability of E occurring at the same time which was to propel the Ibiza scene to new heights.

'I still have an image in my mind of the British kids arriving,' says Alfredo, a former journalist who'd left his homeland when his country was taken over by the right-wing military in the 1970s. 'I've got this picture of them going absolutely crazy; trying to dance inside the speakers, even.' Who could that have been?

Trevor Fung knows. 'It was the funniest sight when we took them all to Amnesia,' he

recalls. 'Danny was shaking his head like mad, climbing inside the speakers. Johnny was skipping around. Paul just looked gobsmacked, and Nicky Holloway, God know what he was doing.'

Alfredo had been developing his sound since starting work at Amnesia in 1984. 'Balearic beat', as it became known, took in everything from raging house tunes to reggae, indie, psychedelia and world music, making for a warm, exhilarating set through which he intended to reach as many diverse people as possible.

'Although I had a fucking massive ego, at the same time, I didn't want to be the usual kind of DJ who thinks he's so cool and important,' Alfredo laughs. 'I wanted my music to welcome in all the people of the world. I wanted to be something different.'

This he was. Though Cesare De Melero, the DJ at the Ku club (now Privilege), was devising a similar sound, it was Alfredo who had perfected it.

'We got into the pattern of Alfredo's music.' says Fung. 'It was fantastic. We got to know his set off by heart that summer.'

'His music was like a rollercoaster ride,' adds Walker. 'Some of it was commercial, some of it was totally underground: there'd be Chicago house, then Madonna, then a dance mix of INXS. For us, with our backgrounds in soul, jazz and hip-hop, this was an incredible experience.'

So incredible that their plans to take it easy for the rest of the holiday were swiftly scuppered. They were to take E and visit Amnesia, Ku and Pacha every night.

'We'd start off each evening at Cafe Del Mar, listening to Jose Padilla's [ambient] music and watching the sun go down,' Walker remembers. 'We'd meet up with other people who'd got into the clubbing. There were no more than a 100 of us from Britain at the time; people like Lisa Loud and Nancy Noise; mainly people from south London. We'd sit there wondering what the night had in store – and we soon realised it was going to be really hard to go home after a week like that.'

Trevor Fung had tried to put on an Ibizan-style party in Purley in 1984. It was called Funhouse, yet it didn't turn out to be much fun.

'Nobody understood what was going on,' he laments. 'They didn't appreciate the colourful drapes, and the music chopped and changed too much for them. I think the drugs had a lot to do with it.'

Or the lack of them, more accurately. This was to change as E became easier to purchase in 1987. The delirious effects of MDMA, coupled with a trailblazing crowd (from places like Carshalton and Croydon, deep in the south London suburban sprawl) now well-versed in the Ibizan experience, meant there was little stopping Fung and Oakenfold, as they transformed their Streatham hip-hop club, The Project, into a Balearic bash. Soon they'd started Spectrum at Heaven, where Ibizan-style clubbing was promoted on a grand scale, in front of 1,000 eager punters every Monday night, with Johnny Walker one of the DJs. Rampling's Shoom night, the famed seething pit of jubilant hysteria and flouro colours

Alfredo

Mopeds - the only way to travel in Ibiza

Plane passing over Space

which took place at the Southwark Fitness Centre, was also up and running by then. Come the summer of 1988, when the acid house phenomenon was scorched across the UK psyche, Nicky Holloway was cranking up the mayhem several more degrees with his Sin night at the Astoria, the first major weekend rave to take place in the West End.

'Though house music had already surfaced in London, it took the energy we'd discovered in Ibiza to really change clubbing,' believes Fung. 'The colour, the enthusiasm, the love of partying, the fact it was all right to let your hair down, wear bright clothes, and do what whatever you wanted – these things were all so new at the time. Though we begrudgingly accepted we could never have weather as good as in Ibiza, we reckoned we could have the rest of it.'

But while acid house sent shockwaves across the UK, back in the Balearics life altered little. Ibiza, the island formerly known as Ibosim, Albusim, Ebusim, Ebesos, Ebysos, Pitiuses, Ebusus, Yebisah and – still favoured by the locals today – Evissa, had seen it all before. It's well documented that the only thing which has prevailed across its 570-square kilometres of beautiful beaches, tranquil hills and sun-baked plains more than endless warring (hence the many names it's acquired over the years) is a fond taste for hedonism. It's an art which the Romans and Carthaginians took to keenly in days of yore. And though the island's officials opted to back General Francisco Franco, the right-wing dictator who came to power in 1936, after Spain's horrendous civil war, Ibiza clung tight to its liberal soul this century. Gay people flocked to the tolerant island in the 1950s, followed by myriad hippies, including Americans dodging the Vietnam War.

In *Hippie Hippie Shake*, *Oz* magazine editor Richard Neville's memoirs of the 1960s, there's talk of wild full-moon parties on the island, with folk singer Donovan and feminist writer Germaine Greer among the notable attendees; of people 'floating free' on a 'jewel of decadent splendour'.

It was therefore situation normal in Ibiza, with the regular tourists largely remaining in San Antonio and, give or take the odd adventurous Brit, Europe's most flamboyant characters having Ibiza Town and the clubs to themselves. The full-scale invasion of British clubbers and promoters was still some way off, but people were at least trying to set it in motion: Nicky Holloway had taken his Special Branch club to Ibiza in 1988; Tommy Mac had done the same with Passion in 1989. Yet both of these were small-scale happenings, attracting around 100 people a time. The event which linked the early period of clubbing on Ibiza to today's huge infiltration of UK promoters was Flying's Ibiza '90 sojourn. Organised by Charlie Chester, now a major player in club promotion, the idea was to haul the rabid spirit contained within their weekly session at the Soho Theatre to Ibiza for two weeks. DJs Andy Weatherall, Terry Farley, Dean Thatcher, Orde Meikle, Stuart McMillan, Phil Perry, Rocky & Diesel, Darren Emerson and Fabio Paras duly arrived on the island in early June. As did live acts The Farm, 808 State and A Man Called Adam, and 600 buoyant punters. Then the uber-messiness began...

Atlantis

'Back through time something has drawn people to Ibiza,' reasons Chester. 'People would stop off there and get wankered for a couple of days on the way home from a war. We were just continuing that tradition, except without the war, obviously.'

Chester rightfully believes this event was a precursor for things to come, but admits that at times it seemed they'd bitten off more than they could chew.

'We were stupid enough to try and organise everything. I'd be in Ku at six in the morning, the whole place would be going mad and suddenly somebody would go, "Oi! What about the dripping tap in my apartment? When's it going to get fixed?" And I'd reply, "Your fucking tap?! What about my head? I'm all over the shop! Go away!"'

Cheerfully oblivious to such organisational horrors, Dean Thatcher, now of The Aloof, simply remembers a giddy mix of fantastic music and great times.

'My most vivid recollection is Weatherall dropping Primal Scream's "Come Together" at Ku,' he says. 'None of us had ever heard it before and the timing was perfect. Everyone was coming up, this projection of a spider's web was creeping across the walls and it was like, "Fucking hell! Spontaneous combustion time!"'

Moments of this kind were laid bare for folk who'd never even been to the island when *A Short Film About Chilling*, a documentary covering the Ibiza '90 trip, was shown in August

Sunset at Anjuna

Cafe Del Mar

of that year on Channel 4. Produced and directed by Kevin Sampson, then The Farm's manager, it scored among one of the highest viewing figures achieved by a youth show on Channel 4 at that time. Needless to say, it played a major role in introducing the UK's still nascent club scene to the joys of the White Island.

'Even now people come up to me and say, "You were on that documentary, weren't you?"' smiles Chester. 'It's impossible to put into words the influence it's had on people.'

And so, while paying respect to your elders isn't normally all it's cracked up to be, this tale plainly highlights one grand exception to the rule. Courtesy of four lads embarking on seven nights of clubbing, chilling and yet more clubbing, a fantastical blueprint had been laid in place, and as the other chapters of this book will explain, it was to be followed with breathtaking gusto.

Ibiza all-time dancefloor top ten

1 SEX MACHINE James Brown
2 AIN'T NOBODY Chaka Khan
3 GOING BACK TO MY ROOTS Richie Hancius
4 EXODUS LIVE Bob Marley
5 LET THE MUSIC USE YOU Nightwriters
6 RAPPER'S DELIGHT Grandmaster Flash
7 JUST CAN'T GET ENOUGH Depeche Mode
8 THE BOTTLE Gil Scott Heron
9 SYMPATHY FOR THE DEVIL The Rolling Stones
10 THE LOVE I LOST Harold Melvin and the Blue Notes

Jose Padilla, Cafe Del Mar

▷ **Jose Padilla, Cafe Del Mar resident DJ:** 'Twenty-five years ago, Ibiza was a paradise. It was very wild and free. It was the first place where I saw so many people from different countries sitting around the same table talking. In Ibiza, you don't have to fight like you do in a city. Nobody takes any notice of you as long as you don't give them any trouble.'

8am – waiting outside Ku for the disco bus

▷ **Duane Dawson, A&R distribution/clubber:** 'I first went in 1988 with friends from Shoom and I had no idea what to expect. I was amazed. I couldn't believe how open everybody was to drugs. The people on the island had obviously been into it for a long time and that's why there was such a strong vibe there. The first night we went to Amnesia and the club was unreal. We walked in there, bought some drugs and went straight to the dancefloor for the duration. Amnesia was great because you felt so comfortable in there – you could relax and let the night flow. The club was unlike anything, and I'd been clubbing many years before that in London. I went back a year later for the opening of Amnesia with 35 friends and that night will always be the best night I've ever had in a club.'

▷ **Nick Hanson, clubber, on Ibiza:** 'I've been going there as a kid since 1972 and all I remember of beaches like Sa Trincha is loads of chilled people sitting in straw huts with bloody long hair! And then in the 1980s it went all peroxide and everybody looked like they were from the band Europe. I'll never forget dancing in Space at 11 am and up popped my dad on the dancefloor. And what annoyed me the most was that he'd blagged it in for free and I had to pay! That's when I knew my dad was a real chap. Ibiza is simply the blueprint for all hedonism. An entire island fuelled on ecstasy tablets. You still can't beat it.'

Duane Dawson (left) and Nick Hanson

Martyn Passey, Ibiza clubber in 1989: 'My best and worst memory is standing outside Amnesia, which had no roof, without tickets. A fight started at the front of the queue among English people and when we finally got to the front they knocked us back. We were gutted. We could see the club starting to kick off over the walls and it was the worst feeling ever. We went back a few days later and it was fabulous. I also remember coming out of a club and allowing a certain DJ to ride my bike without realising he was tripping out of his head! We went on a scrambling ride down to the Cafe Del Mar. I then remember standing in a baker's shop waiting for custard donuts whilst holding paper flowers and thinking it was the most natural thing in the world. And also being at Cafe Del Mar and vowing one day I would work there. And later on I did.'

The disco bus

Phat Phil Cooper and Rosanna Maldonado

▷ **Rosanna Maldonado, Ibizan club promoter:** 'I've spent five summers in Ibiza and I love it because people, no matter who they are, lose all their airs and graces when they get out there. People have a great time and get on with people of all nationalities under the one roof. I love the contrast of the island – the commercial and the not-so commercial side. And yes, Ibiza is magical. I haven't read about it, but I've heard rumours about the lay lines underneath the island. I'm a strong believer in this, and I sincerely believe its a magical place.'

Eirik The Viking, original British Ibiza clubber: 'I first went there on my own for the closing in September 1988. I met somebody who turned out to be a real character and he took me on the most amazing tour of every bar, club and restaurant on the entire island. He got me into all the clubs for free and introduced me to amazing people like Brazillio from Ku and a host of freaks. It was a life-changing moment. It really is a magical place and it truly takes you beyond anything you'd ever experience, certainly in terms of hedonism. You find out so much about yourself in Ibiza and that's the maxim I come out with – Ibiza touches every part of you. If you treat it right, it treats you right. It's not called the magic island for nothing. Atlantis, where the big rock is, is a complete spiritual energizer and you couldn't get further away from San An. The combination of people makes it like nowhere else in the world.'

Ku Club, 1990

◁ **Sue Bennison, Loco Motive holiday company:** 'I've lived and worked in Ibiza for 15 years. I went there as a holiday rep and all I knew was that I would be staying somewhere in the Mediterranean. As time later proved, luckily enough I ended up in Ibiza. I fell in love with the place instantly. I love the island itself, the people, the culture, the climate and, yes, the nightlife is a major part of it because the whole island is nocturnal. Having spent time at Amnesia and Ku in the early days, I still find myself being dragged back year after year for more of the same. My lifestyle is fabulous in Ibiza. It does still feel different here because of the collection of people from all over the world. It's such a happening place. People come for the club scene essentially, but when they're here they become creative and inspired and end up doing something really positive as a result. I get so much satisfaction from seeing the results of these things and watching them develop. Whatever new generations of people come through, the roots are still here and the people are still living their lives as usual.'

▷ **Brazillio, owner of Ku, on the Ibiza vibe:** 'Because the Ku club was an open-air discotheque people thought that was the importance of the place. But the importance is Ibiza, the island. Its whole history is of a very tolerant place. Ibiza was a place where anybody who didn't agree with the system used to come and visit. If you read about the Phoenicians and the whole history of the island, what they used to do here is stranger than what is happening now. Ku club is the mirror of Ibiza. Everything happening in Ibiza you can see here on the dancefloor. It is the new temple of Ibiza.

A Short Film About Chilling, Channel 4, 1990

Ibiza all-time chill-out top ten

1 MOMENTS IN LOVE Art of Noise
2 EVERYBODY LOVES THE SUNSHINE Ramp
3 ONCE UPON A TIME IN AMERICA Enio Morricone
4 METRO RODRIGO Concierto Aranjuet
5 EASY WAY OUT Praise
6 WISH YOU WERE HERE Pink Floyd
7 JUAO GILBERTO Gilberto & Getz
8 ARE YOU GOING WITH ME? Pat Metheny
9 FANFARE OF LIFE Leftfield
10 AGUA Jose Padilla

Jose Padilla, Cafe Del Mar

Bez from the Happy Mondays, on discovering Ibiza: 'At Pacha, it took me a whole week's worth of visits to work out that I'd been usin' the girls' khazies, liberally slappin' on all the perfumes and lotions without payin', much to the delight of the attendant who I later realised was a screamin' transvestite. I thought at the time that they were bein' very generous puttin' out all this after-sun stuff for the poor, ravaged, baked an' peelin' clubbers like myself. I hadn't realized also that the podiums were there solely for the paid dancers. Every night I was flingin' myself up there, grinnin' away like a madman an' they never once tried to throw me off. Don't know why.'

Freaky Dancin' by Bez, Pan Books

◁ **Simone Angel, former MTV presenter, on Ibiza in 1989:** 'I lost my virginity there in more ways than one! I was just 16 and if I hadn't made that trip from Amsterdam, I would never have joined MTV and ended up doing what I'm doing. I moved to England to be closer to the culture I experienced in Ibiza. It just blew my mind, and I desperately wanted to be a part of it. I loved the madness and the complete anarchy about the place. At 16 I hadn't seen much of life and what I witnessed was these freaks running around Ibiza wearing stupid bandannas and smiley t-shirts. It seemed such a good way to rebel. I moved to England and stayed in a youth hostel and went to every club listed in **Time Out**. Of course Ibiza is different now, but the madness is still there. I compare it to deep-sea diving in that when you go underwater all your senses are gone, you don't know which way is left or right and you've no idea how long you've been under the water. It's the same thing in Ibiza. You don't know whether you should eat, sleep or party. And the beauty is, it doesn't matter.'

Danny Rampling at Amnesia

△ **Danny Rampling on discovering the Ibiza vibe:** 'We walked into Amnesia and that was the moment my life changed irrevocably. The music was mind-blowing. The set Alfredo was putting together was pure inspiration. American tunes mixed with European sensibilities made Amnesia a melting pot where anything could happen. It was the Paradise Garage of Europe. The human energy was amazing. Our time had come and we knew this was a magical thing which had to be shared.'

Pacha

chapter three

Ibiza the British invasion

By Andy Pemberton

'I WAS UNDER THE IMPRESSION THAT KU WAS THIS GREAT CLUB AND WE WERE JUST living in the shadow of its glorious past,' avers club supremo Andy Manumission. 'It's that argument – it's not as good as it used to be. Then you started talking to people and you realised, actually it never was this good. This was as fantastic as it had ever been. This was the dream of the people who had built Ibizan clubs like Ku and Amnesia. But they'd never actually made it. Until we came along.'

It was Manumission's end of the season party in 1994 when Andy Manumission first realised Ibizan clubbing had gone into overdrive. For the first time in years, Ku, that gargantuan, 8,000-capacity barn that swallowed up so many ambitious promoters in the past, was packed.

'In the space of a few months we'd gone from getting 500 people through the door to 7,000,' sighs Andy. 'That was amazing.' And it wasn't just Manumission that was rammed.' Liverpool superclub Cream, installed on Thursday nights at the same venue, was the second club spearheading Ibiza's clubbing renaissance.

'It was phenomenal,' boggles Cream supremo James Barton. 'The first time we did Ku in 1994, there were something like 10,000 people outside screaming to get in.'

According to the Ibizan tourist authority, 593,500 Britons travelled to Ibiza that summer – many of them youthful clubbers. By 1996, the figure reached 623,000. That's almost twice the amount of holiday makers who made the trip in 1992.

Manumission

Es Paradis

Pacha

As a cultural phenomenon too, Ibiza had arrived. It was no longer an island but a way of life. Ibiza was broadcast on UK radio, printed on t-shirts and emblazoned on the covers of dozens of CD compilations. Between 1994 and 1996 Ibiza turned from a noun to an adjective. You could even pronounce it differently: Ibeefa, innit?

As recently as the early 1990s Ibiza had been attempting to live off its rather tired reputation as the birthplace of modern club culture. In 1987 four London soulboys had taken Ecstasy, and decided to bring the 'vibe' back to a recession-hit UK. Clubbing became the driving force of British youth culture, but out in Ibiza that initial burst of energy had long since dissipated.

Meanwhile, in the minds of hard-up British clubbers, Ibiza was little more than a myth, propagated by misty-eyed DJs, still trapped in that golden moment in 1987 when they danced in roofless clubs to an ad hoc selection of records, spun by Argentinian ex-pat DJ Alfredo. Ibiza was ancient history.

And any clubbers who actually made it out to the island in the early 1990s were forced to agree. James Barton holidayed there in 1992. He wasn't impressed. 'It was funny. It was the back end of the Nicky Holloway, Paul Oakenfold era. I went to a couple of parties run by [West London's] Flying Records at Pacha. It was pretty shite. I thought, "Oh well, I missed that one."'

British promoters such as Black & White and A Clockwork Orange were staging cheap and cheerful nights under cheesy titles like Mad Mondays or Ku Crazy Ku. San Antonio, the island's second major town and package holiday centre, was a riot of burger bars, moped concessions and full English breakfasts. There was Cafe Del Mar, the small, beachfront cafe tucked away at one end of the town where DJs spun mood music as the sun set, and Sa Capella, a secluded restaurant in a monastery on the C'an Germa Road on the way out of town, but not much else. For the most part, San Antonio was comprised of pubs with names like The Londoner and ritzy discos that abruptly cleared when visiting tour parties had to board coaches and head for the next boozy nightspot on their itinerary.

In Ibiza Town, there was still the gay quarter, the old walled city and upmarket clubs like the sparsely populated Pacha. But there was an overriding sense that the best days were long gone. Even as late as 1994, as Andy Manumission arrived at the start of the season, things were still pretty grim.

'Ibiza was in a lull,' he says. 'Most of the island was beautiful but the clubs weren't good. At that time the best club in Ibiza was Space, which started in the early morning. In the nighttime clubs there was nothing happening, there was nowhere great to go.'

That spring, I had visited Cafe Del Mar DJ Jose Padilla at his villa in the pine and fig trees up in the Ibizan hills. The Spanish DJ had fled family troubles in Barcelona in 1974 and, after playing in tourist clubs for a few years, was now the resident at the Cafe Del Mar. He had just finished compiling his first chill-out compilation LP (named after the cafe) and was now trying to organise a series of his Moondance parties at Pacha. The owner was reluctant to commit himself, and Padilla was becoming frustrated. He said he could sense that 1994 could be a good year, but still doubted that even Ibiza's flagship venue Ku, which was beset by organisational problems, would open its doors that summer.

Back in London, Andy Manumission called me asking for some contact numbers for Ibizan club-owners. He'd heard that Ku needed a promoter and he had already quit his club at Manchester's Equinox venue. A local thug who had been refused entry had returned to the venue and poured petrol over him. He threatened to set fire to the promoter.

So, with just that night's door-take, Andy and his brother Mike fled to Ibiza. Believing it to be a less troubled location than Manchester, they soon decided to try to start a club there. They had no idea how easy it was going to be.

'There really wasn't much out there, so the clubs were quite keen to talk to new promoters,' shrugs Andy. 'We were amazed. We had hardly any experience. There were five of us and we were time-sharing two beds. We didn't even have a car. Ku offered us a night every week.'

They ingratiated themselves with islanders too often shunned by cocky British promoters. The kind of parties Manumission were planning to stage would be far more elaborate than those other British-run events. They wouldn't be reliant on DJs, they said, but would place a much greater emphasis on a flamboyant social mix of people. This would chime with Ibiza's libertarian reputation – forged by its unique mix of geography and climate, as well as its history as an easy-going refuge for those deemed undesirable by Franco's fascist government.

Manumission hyped their night by craftily employing an army of British beach bums to flyer tourists and locals alike. Paid by the amount of people they could persuade into the club, their staff were well rewarded for their efforts and, happily, the club was heaving. It was a wildly successful ruse.

'People would get 30 flyers thrust into their hands, and everyone would tell them this was going to be the best night ever,' recalls Andy.

Promising a return to the Balearic ideal of a dionysan excess, they encouraged clubbers to participate in the festivities – dressing up, giving out sweets or sweeping the floor – anything that added up to more than their rivals 'DJs and dodgy decor' combination. They were also surprised to discover that people on the island genuinely wanted Ku to succeed.

'There was a real love of Ku on the island,' explains Andy, 'our numbers doubled in a period of three weeks. It went crazy.'

At the same time, Cream took the plunge and became the first superclub to stage regular nights on the island, gazumping their UK rivals Ministry Of Sound. They'd thrown a one-off party at Pacha the year before but now, encouraged by the dance label Deconstruction, Cream flew in expensive American DJs and had Kylie Minogue play live, immediately outshining nights at San Antonio knees-up joints such as The Star Bar, Extasis or even the long-established foam palace Es Paradis. Cream's presence also lent Ku a vital air of

Manumission

Es Paradis

familiarity. In order to get the kind of numbers needed to kickstart the club, Cream had to attract San Antonio's 18-35 package tourists, who were spooked by rumours that the venue was little more than a temple of homosexual depravity. The source of these scare stories was unlikely to say the least; it wasn't rival promoters, but British holiday reps. Mindful of their club commissions, they set about dreaming up tales of sexual deviancy to persuade youthful British holiday makers to spend their money not in Ku, but in clubs which paid

the reps kickbacks. (In 1998, this practice reached comical proportions when, in an attempt to put off excited British clubbers, it was claimed Manumission sacrificed live goats on stage. Radio One bought it and attempted to follow up the story, but didn't get too far.)

Despite the ridiculous smear campaign, and buoyed by an upturn in the British economy, the end of the 1994 season saw both Manumission and Cream rammed and, as a result, Ibiza's clubbing rebirth in full swing. The following year, Cream relocated to

Amnesia, attracting crowds of 7,000 as well as a pack of hungry British club promoters, who flew out to catch the coat-tails of Cream's success.

Manumission meanwhile, keen to retain their bacchanalian edge, started their live sex show every week.

'We need to be ahead of everyone else and be cutting edge clubbing,' explained Mike, who with girlfriend Claire performed the shows. He outlined his twin-pronged attack: 'We were thinking of dwarves and sex.' On Monday nights, the couple paraded through Ibiza Town's cobbled gay quarter in S&M gear with their new dwarves in tow, and performed girl-on-girl sex in the club, provoking local media outrage as well as plenty of exposure in the papers back home. Unsurprisingly, 1995 proved to be a boom year for Manumission, even though, as Mike quietly reflected, 'It's hard to watch your girlfriend being fucked by another girl. Emotionally, it's quite damaging.'

Over at Cream, James Barton was doing some reflecting of his own.

'By that stage it got ridiculously enormous. We've never put an Ibiza album out but I remember in 1995 talking to Manumission and saying maybe there's a record in this,' he laughs. 'There's nowhere else with records named after it. You wouldn't buy a Sound of Cyprus compilation, would you?'

So why did Ibiza clubbing explode in the mid 1990s? And how has the island managed to keep up the blistering pace ever since? For Andy Manumission, it's the special atmosphere of the island itself.

'It's got the right melting pot,' he argues. 'The ingredients are in Ibiza in a unique manner. Where else can you build a ludicrous nightclub like Ku, which is so big if you put 4,000 people in it, it's still half full?'

'When we were running a club in Manchester, the whole ethos was to have this real party-crazy atmosphere where anything goes and nobody cares. And it was so delicate, so difficult to set that up, we knew the bubble would burst. We came to Ibiza and it was everything we were trying to create in Manchester on a plate. I know it sounds crap but there's a magic. It's indulgence. There's something about the island that just makes clubs better.'

'The early seeds weren't sown in Ibiza,' believes James Barton. 'They were sown back in this country – the second enormous explosion in club culture. Ibiza went down the same road as the UK, maybe just a couple of years later.'

For Andy, whose Manumission empire now includes two bars, a motel, a travel company and a list of employees numbering over 50, one thing is certain.

'1994 was the pivotal year,' he says. 'The late 1980s were the inspiration but it was nowhere near as successful. 1994 was the start of the real British invasion.'

Claire, Manumission

Manumission

▷ **Charlie Chester, promoter, on Ibiza '90:** 'Nicky Holloway had done a party in 1987 in Ibiza taking people over there, but when we did Ibiza '90 we were the first people to take over all our own DJs, bands and 500 clubbers too! We'd built up loads of contacts around the country since '88 and we took people from all over the UK. We had Orde Meikle and Stuart McMillan from Slam in Glasgow, Dean Thatcher, Andy Weatherall, Phil Perry, Darren Emerson, Justin Robertson with The Farm, A Man Called Adam and 808 State live. Plus the 500 people all buying their flights and accommodation through us. It took about six months to organise the two-week trip in June and it's always really quiet around then so we were relying on our crowd, not just locals. We took some journalists out there too and a film crew. The end result was **A Short Film About Chilling** which I still think is the best youth culture film ever made. In fact it's been shown on Channel 4 quite a few times since. We actually used the Ku club, Pacha and Es Paradis while we were out there, and nobody has really done it like that since. Cream and A Clockwork Orange do the whole summer, but not in the same way we did. The Farm playing Ku was massive news at that time and two months later the band were at the top of the charts.'

Charlie Chester (right)

Cream at Ku

UK club promoter overheard talking to one of his workers outside Mambo in 1996: 'Can you take those Miss Moneypennys posters down from over there. We own that tree. That tree has been ours for the last three years. How dare they.'

Andy McKay, Manumission, 1995: 'I'd like to say we will return but, at this stage, who knows? Manumission are the last hope for Ibiza. If we leave, Ibiza has had it. There aren't enough passionate promoters out here and we are by far the most successful. Ask anyone and they'll say that Manumission were Ibiza in 1995.'

'Trouble Hits Ibiza', *Muzik* magazine, September 1995

Amy Thomson, ex Ministry of Sound organiser, on Ibiza: '1998 was my first year and I loved the joining of so many different European people in one place. I love the place because everyone is on such a bloody mission to get the maximum out of their two-week stay that nobody goes to bed. And everybody still looks great because of their suntans. And Pikes hotel is just amazing.'

Ibiza-San Antonio bus

Ministry at Pacha

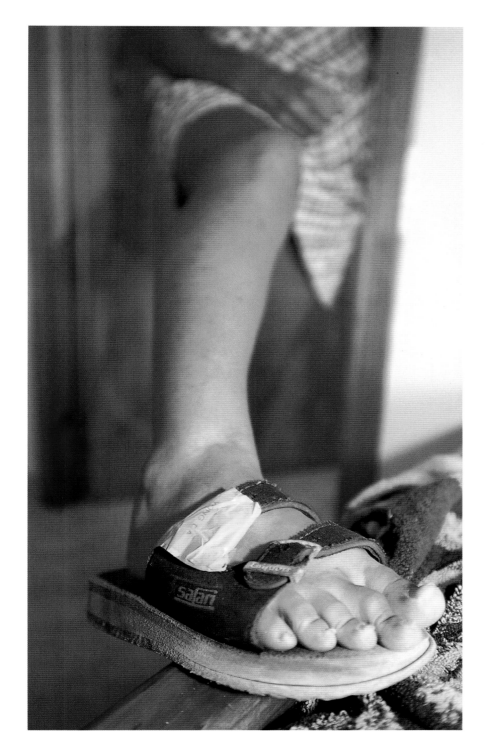

Emma, Ibiza flyerer: 'We originally came to Ibiza with Club 18-30. It was very cheap and they provide the accommodation in advance. I guess it's okay if you're the sort of person who enjoys playing pass the cucumber. If you want to go into San Antonio for a fight, go to shitty clubs like Kaos and throw up a lot, you'll probably like it. But the 18-30 people chucked us out. The maid came in and woke us all up. We were still caned from the night before and we even forgot our stereo when we left. We didn't want to come home, so we managed to find a place in San Antonio. Six of us were sharing and there's only one bedroom. But it's better than the 18-30 dump. We hate the beer-monsters-in-football-shirts mentality you get there. You get that sort down the West End, but not in the clubs we go to, like Pacha, Ku, Amnesia and Space. We're into the right stuff, know what I mean?'

'Wish You Were Here', *Muzik* magazine, October 1996

Gill Nightingale, a Cream worker, on the stress and strain of working on the island all summer: 'It's been hard. We were warned of the problems before coming. We have just learnt not to let things upset us. There have been lots of personality clashes, but before we came here we only knew each other from nights out in Liverpool. When you're working in a close-knit situation like this, you feel guilty even going to lunch without your colleagues. You have to hide when you are eating in case someone sees you! But because we're all working for the same cause, we have to get on. All of us here are suffering stress at the same time, so we all feel fucked off at the same time. When you take a set of people and throw them all in together, of course you're going to get personal problems. The conflicts are over the smallest things, like sharing bathrooms and swapping clothes.'

Amy, worker, on the police: 'The Guardia Civil are lenient when they want to be, but they can be just as quick to stitch you up for nothing. If they find somebody with ten pills on them, they might let them off or they might decide to send them down for ten years. It's a lottery out here.'

'Wish You Were Here', *Muzik* magazine, October 1996

1989 the Ibiza anthems

1 FRENCH KISS Lil' Louis (ffrr)

2 TEARS Frankie Knuckles (ffrr)

3 STRINGS OF LIFE Rhythim Is Rhythim (Transmat)

4 KEEP ON MOVING Soul 2 Soul (D.F.C.)

5 THE REAL LIFE Corporation Of One (Smokin')

6 PACIFIC STATE 808 State (ZTT)

7 THAT'S THE WAY LOVE IS Ten City (Elektra)

8 STORIES Izit (Virgin)

9 RIDE ON TIME Black Box (Lombard)

10 WHY Carly Simon (WEA)

compiled by Pippi – Pacha resident

Sunset at Cafe Del Mar

David Williams, older resident of Ibiza, on life away from the clubs: 'Ibiza is a beautiful place, especially in the winter when there are no tourists here and the beaches are empty. Me and my wife ended up moving here by mistake, after a stay in Australia fell through. I saw an advert for a house for sale and came over to look at it. We didn't buy that one, but we liked the island and soon found somewhere else. What goes on in the rest of the island doesn't really affect our lives. Most of the inhabitants of Ibiza don't get involved in that side, and the clubbers seem to be concentrated in the West End or the areas around Ku and Pacha. And besides, when those people are coming home, the people who I call the "sane people" are all in bed. So many of the clubbers sleep most of the day and lounge around by the pool and then they're off again for another night out and they never see the real island. They go home and think they've had a good time and all they saw was the West End and one of the clubs. The people who come for the scenery either move here or keep coming back. At this time in the season the wild orchids are amazing. The clubbers can't even face a 30-minute ferry to Formentera, whose beaches are as stunning as some of those around the Barrier Reef. These kids have probably never seen anything like it in their lives and yet they're too pissed and hungover to face the journey. It's around December that the clubbers should visit Ibiza and experience how amazing the island really is.'

1990 the Ibiza anthems

1 LFO LFO (LFO)
2 YOU GOT THE LOVE Candi Staton (Virgin)
3 ELEVATION Expansions (Deconstruction)
4 THE POWER - CULT OF SNAP Snap (Logic)
5 GROOVE IS IN THE HEART Dee-Lite (Elektra)
6 CHIME Orbital (ffrr)
7 THE MASTERPLAN Diana Brown & Barry K Sharpe (ffrr)
8 SHELTER ME Circuit (Cooltempo)
9 REACH UP TO MARS Heart People (Nu Groove)
10 THE THEME Unique 3 (Talkin' Loud)

compiled by Pippi — Pacha resident

Rob Da Bank, journalist, on Ibiza's West End: 'We drag our sorry arses onto the bus heading for San Antonio, the Las Vegas of Ibiza. The cheapest part of the island to look for hotels/drugs/sex, San An's beer glasses are plastic, the chips are hollow oblongs of fat and the town centre contains the highest percentage of football shirts and sunburnt necks per square kilometre this side of Bognor Regis. Perfect. Lugging out toothbrushes through the centre of San An, we're heartened to see Union Jacks hanging from balconies, fish 'n' chip shops every five yards and cafes advertising "Pints 500 Ptas". Our hotel is rammed with Brits abroad so we join in being rude to the receptionist, ordering pork scratchings at the bar and throwing glasses into the pool.'

'Slumming It In Ibiza', *Muzik* magazine, September 1998

The Ship Inn

San Antonio

Renaissance's Geoff Oakes (left) and Austin Wilde

◁ **Austin Wilde, worker for Renaissance, on the Guardia Civil:** 'In 1996 I was resident DJ and head of the Renaissance PR team working on the island, and I was pulled over while driving Paul Oakenfold across the island. He was sitting in the back. I was taken to a local bank and made to withdraw my £250 daily limit. They then kicked me in the stomach after I had handed all the money over.'

◁ **Geoff Oakes, Renaissance MD, on the relationship with Spanish clubs:** 'The deals being struck between the clubs always fall in favour of the islanders. I'm sure the club owners get together every year and decide how they're going to make more money. We're outlaying a massive amount on our workers with little return. We're just filling the club for Pacha.'

A Clockwork Orange

Manumission

Manumission

Manumission

1991 the Ibiza anthems

1 FAITH Rozalla (Virgin)
2 NOT FORGOTTEN Leftfield (Hard Hands)
3 GO Moby (Virgin)
4 ALRIGHT Urban Soul (Circuit)
5 GENERATE POWER Photon Inc (Strictly Rhythm)
6 FINALLY Ce Ce Penniston (A&M)
7 WHAT WOULD WE DO DSK (Boy's Own Production)
8 PLAYING WITH KNIVES Bizarre Inc (Virgin)
9 THE PRESSURE Sounds Of Blackness (A&M)
10 SUCH A GOOD FEELING Brothers In Rhythm (4th & Broadway)

compiled by Pippi – Pacha resident

▷ **Rob Da Bank, journalist, on the West End:** 'After sundown we join the herd marching up and down the West End. One long riotous street with smaller riotous ones going off it. Every other building is a free nightclub, fake Tudor pub or chip shop. It's like Middlesbrough, only smaller. Most people here aren't interested in the big-name clubs and who can blame them when you can get into one of any ten clubs for free, hear identical tunes to those played by the big names and get a free shot of schnapps every time you buy a beer or spirit. The basic idea seems to be to get through as many drinks as possible, leer at girls and pass out with your face in a plate of chips and gravy. Seems rude not to join in. By 3am there are truckloads of people going by in buses singing "Vindaloo" even though England has just been knocked out of the World Cup. The last thing I remember is dropping my pizza crust in the sand and then eating it through gritty teeth.'

'Slumming It In Ibiza', *Muzik* magazine, September 1998

Dave Fowler, journalist, on his spiritual Ibiza: 'Brits go on holiday to Ibiza for a variety of reasons. Some have gone for years, because Thomas Cook tells them to, it's sunny, and you can get egg and chips from a waiter who speaks English. Others, of a more tie-dyed inclination, have heard the island's bedrock is made of quartz, a medium ideally suited to receiving alien messages. Hence the high incidence of UFO sightings in the Balearics. Apparently. A more recent generation has bought heavily into the myth of a Mediterranean clubland nirvana for beautiful people. Propagated by melodic ambient compilations and easily-led journalists on music-biz junkets, the White Island has transmuted from a package holiday destination into a palm-fringed Iberian paradise. Think topless babes lolling around passing gin palaces captained by cocaine-snorting Euro hunks with washboard stomachs and perfect tans. For good measure, add the odd house record (nothing too heavy, mind). Throw in a few pills and it even becomes a bit spiritual. "Spiritually Ibiza!", know what I mean, mate?'

'Wish You Were Here', *Muzik* magazine, October 1996

Thomas Foley, React Records, highlights the absurd club wars in Ibiza:
'When we arrived, we were given a Ford Fiesta instead of the Citron ZX we were promised. We were told we could upgrade the car at our own expense, that we had to pay for the car ourselves and Manumission would repay us the next day. I knew they were having financial problems in Ibiza because we'd heard that they're being screwed by Ku's management. And then our money failed to turn up. I'd been in Ku for five hours and only eight drink tickets were given to any of the React crew. There were 8,000 people in Ku and they were selling a coke at £5. I spent £1,000 at the bar entertaining the people I had brought over with me. If React do Ibiza again, we want £10,000 in advance. I won't be dicked around.'

'Trouble Hits Ibiza', *Muzik* magazine, September 1995

Ku Club

chapter four

Ibiza the music

By Frank Tope

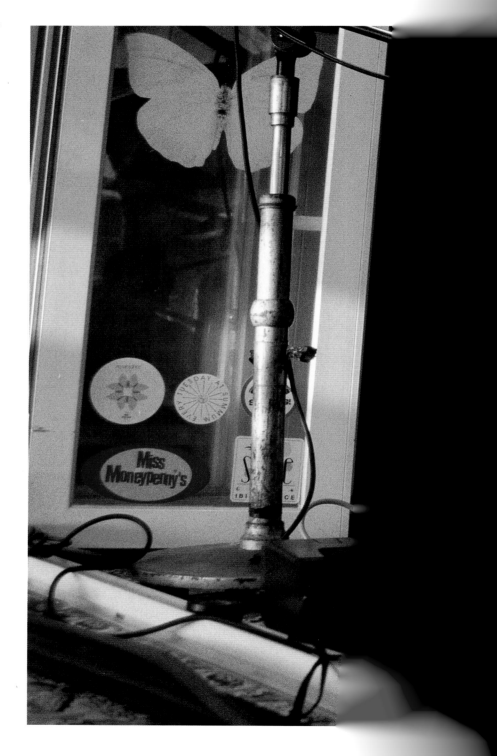

MUSIC SOUNDS BETTER IN IBIZA. SORRY, BUT IT'S TRUE. REMEMBER LISTENING TO Stardust out there? For me it was on the Terrace at Space, July 1998. That familiar guitar riff chiming in. It isn't? It is. We're liberally sprinkled with Stardust, not once, or twice, but three whole times in a row. Quite frankly it doesn't seem long enough. The crowd consists of spangly club freaks from all over Europe, a fair sprinkling of nutted ravers from the night before and the very cream of Europe's DJs and club promoters. All whooping with joy, all willing the now to roll on forever. Six months and over a million copies later the same record is in the pop charts. A great record, no doubt about that. But it never sounded as good back home as it did in Ibiza. Every year there's one or two records from the holiday season that magically turn into enormous chart hits in Britain. This year it was the turn of Thomas Bangalter and friends. The year before it was the Euro-trance stomp of BBE. Before that it was the turbo-funk basslines Armand Van Helden grafted onto Tori Amos' 'Professional Widow' and CJ Bolland's 'Sugar is Sweeter'.

'In Britain,' says veteran DJ Terry Farley, 'records stay in a DJ's box for a month. In Ibiza the DJs will be caning the record all summer.'

Add in the fact everyone's on holiday, losing it on pills, powders and San Miguel for a solid fortnight. Whenever you're not in a club or bar having the time of your life, you're getting ready, preparing for the next chemical assault you're going to visit on your system. If there's an anthem unifying the diaspora of DJs playing on the island, then you're going

Judge Jules at Mambo

Pacha

to hear it more times, in a more 'relaxed' situation, during that fortnight than you would in six months back home. And everyone wants a souvenir from their holiday, and you can't exactly bring a Mitsubishi back with you.

It's nothing new: back in the dark hairspray-soaked days of the mid 1980s, forgettable European disco pop records like Spagna's 'Call Me' or 'Boys Boys Boys' by Sabrina became novelty hits on the back of their anthem status in 18-30 nightclubs across the Med from Majorca to Cyprus. The music isn't what draws people to Ibiza. It's the sun, the sex, the clubs, the drugs. The music just provides a soundtrack to your holiday, then later to your memories. Because the music mightn't be what drew you to the island, but sometimes it just sounds better there.

'The club systems are so good here, you can hear records you don't really like, but hear them the way they were really meant to sound,' says Sally Rogers, singer with A Man Called Adam, a British band that have clasped the Balearic ideal firmly to its bosom. 'You can walk into Pacha and hear Sash! and go, "Oh yeah! That's great!" But if you went to the Ministry and heard it you'd say, "Oh God, that is so depressing!"'

'Music is altered by the environment you hear it in,' says Ibizan DJ Jose Padilla. 'And some music does sound very good here.'

'Of course people like the music in Ibiza!' is the view of popular British DJ Brandon Block, cutting straight to the heart of the matter. 'You're in the sun! Everyone's on holiday!'

'The music has always been bad in Ibiza,' mutters Terry Farley darkly. 'It didn't matter, it was the place that made it.' Back when Terry and his Boys Own compadres first visited Ibiza in 1988, the music spun by DJs like Cesar De Melero in Pacha and Alfredo in Amnesia was a mix of pop, rock and dance music, all played by one or two DJs all night.

'The best night of my life,' says Farley, 'was the opening night of Amnesia in 1989. Alfredo played "Pump Up The Jam" by Technotronic six times that night. People knew the record was rubbish – but it didn't matter. The place and the vibe was so good it didn't matter if you were dancing to Phil Collins at ten in the morning. It was brilliant then. It doesn't really wash now, of course.'

What drew the early Balearic fans to clubs like Ku and Amnesia wasn't the music played by DJs like Alfredo. It was the spectacle, the sense of occasion, of oiks gatecrashing a millionaire's playground. As Farley puts it, 'These clubs were like Stringfellows really, with rich European trendies rather than English working-class people who had gone to hear house music.'

'We played disco stuff, new romantic, a bit of rock, a bit of reggae. Everything really,' says Jose, who has been DJing on Ibiza since the 1970s. 'It was a bit of a surprise for the English to hear all these different musics. And the environment makes them pay more attention to the music.'

And when the English were exposed to the mixture of records, there's no doubt that for some it was a revelation. When early Ibiza club converts Trevor Fung and Paul Oakenfold

Amnesia dancer

attempted to play their Ibizan pop-edged mix of music to their soul-boy crowd back in London in 1985, the reaction was nothing short of bemusement. But three years later, with the covert addition of MDMA, the imported mixture was set to become the biggest youth cult Britain has seen.

DJs like Jose claim that Ibiza's music stopped being individual with the onset of house music and the rave culture exported en masse by British clubbers. But the vibe has remained the same. It's just that DJs from all over Europe have thrown in their influences to the island's potent mix. The first wave of organised British holidays was in 1990, when Charlie Chester's Flying organisation brought over British DJs like Andrew Weatherall to play the current mellow London interpretation of the 'Balearic' sound.

'All kinds of people were on the bill – Farley, Rampling, Weatherall, Rocky & Diesel, Steve Bicknell, Dean Thatcher,' recalls Glaswegian DJ Orde Meikle of Slam. 'But most of them were really into the downbeat stuff like Maureen Walsh's "Thinking of You" and Saint

Etienne's "Only Love can Break Your Heart". It was really only me and Andy playing anything housey or techno.'

The first British DJ to really set out his stall on the island wasn't from the cool Balearic clique. It was north Londoner Alex P.

'When I first went to Amnesia,' says the long-time Ibiza DJ, 'the records Alfredo was playing were really cheesy. Italian house, stuff like Black Box's "Ride On Time". I started my own night playing UK warehouse music: techno, garage, industrial sounding records like Fallout's "The Morning After" and The Nightwriters' "Let the Music Use You". DJs like Oakey used to go over there and take from the island's music. I said. "Fuck it, I'm going to play UK-style music."'

As a result of the influence of Brits like Alex and equally pro-active German DJs like Sven Vath and Mark Spoon, by 1992 there was a split in the island's music, that has remained established to today. Many of the clubs in the island were deviating from the original

David Morales filming for the 1998 Ibiza smash 'Needin' U'

Balearic holiday sound and playing the hard European techno pioneered by labels like R&S and producers such as Frank De Wulf and Joey Beltram. The differing styles of music were particularly apparent on Sunday mornings at beach-side after-hours club Space.

'I used to say it was Heaven and Hell,' says Alex P. 'Inside was hell: mad industrial techno and strobes. Outside was heaven. I started playing outside on the Terrace for all the transvestites who'd been out all night and wanted some fun and games music. We played house, a lot of older stuff, hip hop. A bit like an old roadshow!'

With the success of UK-promoted clubs like Manumission and Cream in 1995 came a fresh deluge of British DJs. Chuffed to bits to be playing on their culture's spiritual home, but still with their own musical agenda to push. The records that started to explode on Ibiza's dancefloors were nothing new to British clubbers, just the anthems they had already got used back home. There's no doubt that it was Ibiza that helped push Josh Wink's 'Higher Sate of Consciousness' or Tori Amos' 'Professional Widow' to the top of the British charts, but they did already have the benefit of months on the UK's own underground.

Last year, 1998, seemed different. Perhaps not because of a sea change in the Ibizan clubbing climate, although the Italian influx into clubs like Ministry of Sound's nights at Pacha have helped the acceptance of black American-influenced club music, but because of the hard house sounds pushed by DJs like Tall Paul and Seb Fontaine back home in Blighty. The US garage-influenced records that many of the DJs loved – Stardust, David

Morales' 'Needin' U' – were simply too lightweight and slow to be anthems at the big UK nights like Gatecrasher and Golden. But they sounded perfect in Ibiza. Garage records too slow to work in big clubs up North getting a chance to shine in the sun.

Perhaps house music is big and clever enough these days for people to get into garage one night then banging Euro trance the next. Certainly the dominance of French and US disco grooves didn't dent the popularity of massive European records like Energy 52's hardy perennial 'Cafe Del Mar' or Nalin and Kane's 'Beachball'.

Or perhaps everyone just needs a little nonsense in their lives, especially on holiday. In 1998 Trade and Carwash, two of London's most popular nights, took up Ibizan residencies. One known for furiously hard gay techno, one for self-parodying 1970s disco revivalism. Each providing cheerfully mindless music in its own way – but both making perfect (non)sense for holidaying Brits, rather than in darkened urban clubs.

Of course, full-frontal club tunes aren't the only music to have been popularised by Ibiza. Jose Padilla's long-running residency at the San Antonio seaside bar Cafe Del Mar was the most high-profile reflection of the ambient chill-out music favoured by many more mature clubbers.

'Ibiza's great when you're 18,' says Sally Rogers, 'all you want to do is go clubbing and shagging 24 hours a day. Horny horny horny. But it's also great when you're a bit older and you want to relax in the ambient cafes. The best Ibizan music is all about dope beats, soft padded strings, a cinematic feel, very evocative of sunrises and sunsets. All the things Ibiza's famous for. Oh, and nice birds singing and people muttering in Spanish.'

She should know: A Man Called Adam contributed two now classic tracks to Jose's 'Cafe Del Mar' compilation series. For many British clubbers these albums, with their warm, sun-kissed ambient feel, gave them an idealised aural vision of what it was like to be in Ibiza.

'Those albums were tremendously important,' says journalist Andy Pemberton. 'The only time I've ever heard music so in tune with its environment was with West Coast hip-hop in LA. The music fitted the environment perfectly. It immediately made you want to go there.'

Although Ibizan DJs like Jose would maintain that the resident Spanish DJs have been overly influenced by their British colleagues, much of the dance music most feted in Britain has never found a foothold in Ibiza. Big beat, deeper techno and drum & bass, for example is all relegated to guest spots in the back rooms, a sop to media cred. The Chemical Brothers recalled for *The Face* the time they played at Cream in Amnesia. People were coming to them, crying, begging them to stop ruining their holiday with their music! Although Terry Farley maintains that the student fanbase for music like Fatboy Slim will never go to Ibiza, A Man Called Adam's Steve reckons 'rainy, hard, metallic things don't really suit it there'. Perhaps a bit of both. Either way, it makes sense that the music that'll fill a dingy basement in London would mean next to nothing in an open-air Mediterranean venue.

Or perhaps music just sounds better in Ibiza.

20 all-time Ibiza classics

1 CITY LIGHTS William Pitt

2 MANDY'S THEME Mandy Smith

3 SUENO LATINO Sueno Latino

4 TULLIO DE PISCOPO Stop Bajon

5 NEPA Tony Allen

6 WHO DO YA LOVE? Spider

7 YEKE YEKE Mory Kante

8 SOUS LE SOLEIL (KWANZAA POSSE REMIX) De Bodega

9 TOO MUCH Hong Kong Syndicate

10 WAITING FOR THE SUN DJ Takemura

11 RAP IN AFRICA Crazy Eddy

12 LAND OF HUNGER De Melero

13 YOU AND ME Keytronics Ensemble

14 HOT HOT HOT (FRANCOIS KERVORKIAN REMIX) The Cure

15 HELL OR HEAVEN Lupo

16 HISPANOS IN SPACE Jam & Spoon

17 INDIANA Indiana

18 PRESSURE Richard Wahnfried

19 THE HAWK Marianne Faithfull

20 LET THE MUSIC USE YOU Nightwriters

Sergio, chill-out king

Manumission

Manumission

Space

Orde Meikle, Slam DJ, on Ibiza '90: 'Charlie Chester was looking for some non-London DJs to give the package a proper UK feel. I arrived at Ibiza airport with nowhere to stay, but Charlie and his girlfriend put me up. But that was nothing – Harvey arrived with his record box and one plastic bag, in which he had a pair of swimming shorts and a box of records. It was supposed to be for a week, but he ended up staying there for three. So did I. We all just kind of lost it, having such a great time. The first night, everyone went down to Ku. This was before the roof was built, so it was totally in the open air. We were totally blown away. And then, when the DJ played "Naked in the Rain" by Blue Pearl, it started pouring and thundering. People just started stripping off, girls taking their tops off, getting literally naked in the rain. You see – all that Manumission hedonism is nothing new! That night set the standard. I think what really blew me away about the clubs was the sheer amount of money that had been spent on them. The feeling behind them was like nothing I'd ever seen, that willingness just to invest in the club and the club alone, the thought that went into the decoration. They'd even spent huge money on the sound system – this was back in the days when DJs were usually just thrown into a corner. Here they were worshipped. They DJed in elevated hydraulic DJ boxes. And that respect was something completely new. The freedom was amazing. The availability of drugs – they were prevalent everywhere. Those were the days when you could just sit and have a spliff at the bus stop in front of old women. If I have one abiding memory, it's this. Just sitting in a cafe on the other side of the street from this club Summun at six in the morning, just watching Terry Farley and Dean Thatcher pouring chocolate milk over themselves. It was just non-stop mayhem.'

1992 the Ibiza anthems

1 DO YOU WANT IT RIGHT NOW Degrees Of Motion (Cutting Records)
2 STELLA Jam & Spoon (Sony)
3 PASSION Gat Decor (Virgin)
4 YOU ARE THE BEST THING D-Ream (East West)
5 FUNKY GUITAR TC1992 (Time)
6 CARRY ON Marsha Wash (Sony)
7 20HZ Capricorn (DFC / R&S)
8 GROOVY BEAT DOP (Guerilla)
9 HARDTRANCE ACPERIENCE Hardfloor (Harthouse)
10 FEEL SO RIGHT Solution (Deconstruction)

compiled by Pippi – Pacha resident

Tanit, legendary 60s remnant. Amnesia, 1992

Terry Farley (right)

◁ **Terry Farley, Boys Own DJ, on the Balearic vibe:** 'Ibiza and good music never really went hand in hand, and that was the whole appeal of it. You'd go there and dance to records which you'd never dance to at home. I remember hearing Alfredo playing the theme tune from Hill Street Blues as his last record for the whole summer in 1989, and I came home and played it in Brighton to get the most appalling reception. I remember thinking, "This is a bloody dreadful record." It really is a case of right place, right time.'

Steve Jones, A Man Called Adam: 'The first time we went to Ibiza, I heard so much music. We just found ourselves at home there. It stopped us being cool, made us listen to things we never would have in London. It made us feel differently. It's how I'd like to feel all the time.'

Cream

Johnny Walker, Spectrum DJ, on that fateful holiday to Ibiza: 'It was September 1987, and me, Paul Oakenfold, Danny Rampling and Nicky Holloway all went on holiday to Ibiza. Anyway, we came in contact with E for the first time, went to Amnesia, and of course we had the most amazing time. I thought drugs weren't really for me, but when I saw Nicky and Paul holding hands and skipping around the club I thought, "This doesn't look too bad..." It was a warm summer night and Amnesia then was open air, with a mixture of European jet-setters and a flamboyant Spanish gay crowd. In Amnesia we heard Alfredo playing a mixture of Chicago house cut up with indie tracks by bands like The Woodentops, Thrashing Doves and pop records by artists like Madonna, George Michael and The Cure. He even played bits of late-1980s hip-hop. It was entertaining, a mixed crowd with a broad spectrum of music and we wanted to bring that whole vibe back to London.'

Sergio, Ibizan DJ for eight years: 'Ibiza is such a magical place because a fault line runs straight underneath the island. It's the only place in the entire world where I've experienced such extreme highs and lows. And as I've learnt over the years, achieving that balance between the two is so important. I've seen so many people go insane over there, so you have to learn to keep it under control. The mentality of the music in Ibiza was so great because it was open-minded – you could play any style. But that has all changed now that the island has been taken over by the big English clubs. Pippi and Cesar De Malero still love to do that in their sets, and you can still hear such diversity at Cafe Del Mar and Sa Trincha. But the beauty of Ibiza still is that you still hear music there which you won't hear in London. All the beach parties have been stopped for the last three years, but when they do manage to pull them off they're incredible.'

DJ Scott James on Ibiza '90: 'It's turned from the summer of love to people's lives. And its well worth doing.'

A Short Film About Chilling, Channel 4, 1990

Andy Weatherall on Ibiza '90: 'It's 18-30s with a Gaultier Jacket on really.'

◁ **Tehmina Sunni, DJ/singer/clubber:** 'Not only does Ibiza possess a unique and vibrant atmosphere, it generates an innovative community, bringing forward fresh ideas which maintain the islands position at the forefront of the music scene. I love it so much because I'm deeply into the music scene and experiencing the Ibiza season enables you to see so many different places playing these sounds. It's also a place where I can experience a variety of DJs and learn from their performances. It's all about the different people that come from different cultures and styles and amalgamate into one.'

Keith Mullen, The Farm, on Ibiza '90: 'It was just a huge party for two weeks, living out of bin bags but it was a great period, really optimistic. There's a lot of myths about Ibiza, or so the bloke who put us on at Ku reckons – apparently General Franco used to go there – but for me it's just the wine, women, song and sun. Actually, it was all just like "Caligula", that Roman orgy thing. Our roadies got really fucked off with us all because we were having such a great time, no sleep at all. One morning we got up and they were gone. They'd just booked a pair of tickets back to England and left us a note saying "goodbye". These were hardened roadies, and they couldn't handle it. The ironic thing was that the day before, one of them as wandering round with a t-shirt with "I'm so Happy I Could Shit" written on it. We ended up on the side of a mountain one night at DJ Harvey's villa. We all became members of the cult of Harvey. I was Dr Love for two weeks, and went round giving out sexual advice, if you know what I mean.'

△ **Jonathan Grey, daytime resident at Sa' Trincha cafe:** 'I love it here because of the sense of freedom and independence. I used to DJ at raves and in London, but although I'm now earning less money and playing sets which are four times longer, this is better than anywhere in Britain. It's too intense in the UK. It's a youth market. But I feel young here in Ibiza. I'm still carrying on in my shorts! The best thing about Ibiza is that there's music wherever you go. You definitely don't need to bring a cassette player on holiday with you here.'

◁ **Matthew Easton, clubber:** 'My best memory from Ibiza was walking into Es Paradis for the first time and seeing the decor. It blew me away. Then that night a friend of mine caught the clap. He wasn't too chuffed. The next night at Ku the DJ slapped on "Only Love Can Break Your Heart" by Saint Etienne just as everyone was getting out of the swimming pool. It was just awesome. The music on the island is what makes it so special for me, especially anyone from the Boys Own era of 1989 – Rocky, Diesel, Farley, Heller and Weatherall are the only people who know how to play music on the island.'

Leftfield'sPaul Daley, Phil Mison & Jose Padilla

Ben Turner on Cafe Del Mar in 1995: 'Whether you work to live or live to work, you always need somewhere to fall back on. Somewhere you can escape to, somewhere to recuperate and reassess, somewhere to get a perspective, to get a grip. Somewhere called Cafe Del Mar. It doesn't matter how many sunsets you've seen, each one is more emotionally satisfying than the last. When DJ Phil Mison plays Del Mar anthem, 51 Days' "Paper Moon", someone tells him his music is too shallow. "This is as deep as the ocean," Mison replies. And there you have it. Cafe Del Mar is a spiritual, healing home. We can only thank God for not putting it on Blackpool beach.'

'Sun of God', *Muzik* magazine, August 1995

'Cafe Del Mar
The heart of the island
This is the place I search for...'
'Mental Generation', Cafe Del Mar

Amnesia

es paradis

20 all-time chill-out classics

1 YAWN YAWN YAWN 5th Notional
2 RIDING TO RIO William Orbit
3 A FUNKY SPACE RE-INCARNATION Marvin Gaye
4 SECOND CHANCE Virginia Astley
5 VEGA Penguin Cafe Orchestra
6 CÕEST LA OUATE Caroline Loeb
7 REVIVAL Martine Girault
8 NOCTURNE Night Ark
9 AN ORDINARY LIFE Its Immaterial
10 WAKE UP EVERYBODY Harold Melvin
11 PAPER MOON 51 Days
12 CALLING YOU Jeuetta Steele
13 PAST Sub Sub
14 HYMN OF PRAISE Audio For Movement
15 TAKE IT EASY Kalima
16 ANOTHER TIME Flow
17 BATONGA Angelique Kidjo
18 FRONTERA DEL ELSUENO Rey De Copas
19 DEPARTURE Earth Wind & Fire
20 SUBTLE BODY Fila Brazilia

Phil Mison, chill-out king & former resident at Cafe Del Mar

Pepe, owner of Space

▷ **DJ Pippi, resident at Pacha:** 'Ibiza is Scorpion and I am also a Scorpion which is why I have such a good vibe about the island. In the daytime and nighttime, there is always a special feeling around. It was amazing in the 1980s to see how enthusiastic Paul Oakenfold, Nicky Holloway and Danny Rampling really were. They were the first English people we ever knew in Ibiza, and now it is very different because we have English, Italian and German promoters but that also makes it special today. I'm lucky to work in a club like Pacha because we have the best promoter and the best DJs in the world playing here. Everything in the world changes, and Ibiza has had to do the same. When we first played here it was so much more open-minded and it was the real balearic feel – we could put together any style of music and not just the one house beat all night long.'

chapter five

Ibiza
the
decadence

By Dave Fowler

NOT MUCH HAS CHANGED UNDER THE BALEARIC SUN FOR THOUSANDS OF YEARS. EVEN back in 654 BC, the Phoenicians traversed the Mediterranean from Carthage to Ibiza in search of white tablets to help them on their journey. Sure, the tablets in question were only salt, for keeping food fresh as they sailed along their ancient 'sun route' to the edge of the known world, but that's hardly the point. When the Phoenicians founded the city they called it 'Ibosim', which we now call Ibiza Town, and they brought with them the first wave of a culture of liberalism and hedonism which makes the White Island what it is today.

Take the Phoenician's principal deity, Latipan, for instance, who offered guidance and protection to all who worshipped him. Also known as 'the Bull', this omnipotent, bearded benevolent was a heavy drinker who specialised in getting mullahed at banquets. And he wasn't averse to a spot of the other, either: as a randy young god, he famously went out to sea with a bulge in his tunic, spotted two prehistoric nubiles on a wave, and naturally gave them the choice between becoming his daughters or his wives. They chose the latter, and produced a mere 70 offspring in the desert.

With a drunken philanderer as primus in the pantheon, and immolation standard fare for post-prandial entertainment, it was no wonder the Phoenicians were soon suffering defeat in the Punic Wars at the hands of the fast-expanding Roman Empire. In fact, the Romans, eager to harvest the salt flats of Salinas and build the Balearics' original villas, soon conquered Ibiza and awarded it the privileged status of confederated city.

Space

More interestingly from our point of view, the loved-up Latins also set about introducing their legendary brand of Bacchanalian excess on the already party-friendly natives. Mass drunkenness, swinging, homosexuality, bestiality and ritual slaughter were the order of the day. Let's face it, this was a culture where a poem by Ovid concerning young boys and aniseed-oil-covered leather dildos was the nation's favourite. Where the Emperor at the time enjoyed week-long orgies with men, women, horses and tigers. And where poor sexual performers where thrown to the lions.

With such distractions abounding, it's a matter of small wonder that Pliny the Elder found the time to comment famously that 'sapientia vino obumbratur' (wisdom is overshadowed by wine). Come to think of it, that is perhaps the most fitting footnote to Ibiza's Roman history. Oh, that and the fact that by the time the Romans left, the island's once-huge antelope population was extinct.

Soon afterwards, the Roman Empire itself had gone the way of the antelope, and Ibiza entered the Dark Ages, a dreary time where marauding Byzantines and Saracens provided light relief from heavy sessions on the traditional Ibizan herbal liquor. Then, in 711 AD the Moors invaded from North Africa, and renamed the island Yebisah.

Now, it's commonly accepted that the camel is called 'the ship of the desert' because it's full of Arab semen, and with a reputation like that, the Ibizans were soon keeping a watchful eye on their young sons and household pets. But, to be fair, the Moors were also a relatively enlightened lot who put up some spectacular architecture and let the locals get on with their daily business.

Not that that helped them any when the Christian Spanish 'reconquest' reached the island. The Moors were swiftly put to the sword and driven back to the desert of North Africa, as Spain threw up Catholic churches and entered into its 'Golden Age', a period which largely consisted of butchering thousands of Aztecs, Toltecs and Incas, then stealing their gold.

Apart from the odd Turkish raid, which provoked a rash of fortifications on the island, not much happened in Ibiza until the 1930s. Then, an unsavoury young general called Francisco Franco with a penchant for Nazi Germany and all things fascist, invaded a politically turbulent Spain from the garrison towns of North Africa via the Mediterranean. What ensued was a particularly nasty civil war in which over a million Spaniards were killed. Franco won, and appointed himself dictator.

The Balearics as a whole were anti-Franco, not least because they were Catalan, and the general hated regional diversity, language and culture. In fact, the jackbooted Generalissimo hated anybody who didn't agree with him 100 per cent on anything. Which meant that there were more than a few disaffected Spaniards around... artists, workers, students and the like. Catalonia became something of a haven for them, and Ibiza was no exception. In Ibiza, no one much minded (apart from Franco's own police force, the Guardia Civil) if you harboured left-wing sympathies. Happily, then, something of the

Bar area of Ibiza Town

liberalism that the Phoenicians had first imported to the island was still around. By the 1960s, Spain was looking to boost its economy by investment in tourism, and, under the aegis of the Generalissimo, the country's costas were first developed. Ibiza's position and liberal outlook, though, meant that any 'tourists' who got off the ferry from Barcelona were largely alternative. Most notable of the bunch were the hippies, who arrived with marijuana seeds, ideals of free love, crystal balls, purple ohms and notions of Ibizan spirituality. The hippies mixed in easily with the rather bemused locals, and the two lifestyles have co-existed happily ever since. Many hippies remain to this day, including the 54-year-old Jeremy, who could still be found on the Sa Trincha beach in the summer of 1998.

'Being a hippie is much more than a lifestyle, especially here in Ibiza,' explained Jez.

'Being a hippy is all about accepting a belief system which transcends the social, political and moral norms of any established structure, especially class or government. The way of the hippy is also antithetical to the structure of hierarchies. Out here, we are all equal, and believe in peace to resolve differences. The way to peace is through love and tolerance. Freedom is also essential to our beliefs: it's the paramount virtue. Freedom to do as one pleases at all times. To be a hippy is to be free.'

No surprise that with such emphasis on freedom, free love and not-quite-so-free drugs, by the 1970s Ibiza started pulling in a more bohemian jet-set crowd. One of those who landed in the pursuit of pleasure, then settled, was the man behind Pike's Hotel, the legendary Tony Pike. Tony was an Australian playboy who arrived on the island with

El Divino, Ibiza Town

£70,000 in his pocket and a fire burning in his groin. Soon he had bought a farmhouse and was installing his friends in its rooms for weekends of swinging and/or fine food and wine. Early guests included Gunter Sachs, Lord Cowdray and a slew of society beauties.

Then, in the early 1980s, Pike's biggest break came when Wham! filmed the 'Club Tropicana' video by his hotel pool, with the moustachioed Pike himself starring as a barman. Business boomed and Tony's system of 'relaxed sophistication' – i.e. a) do anything you like, but don't offend anyone, and b) no children allowed! – provided the amoral framework. The halcyon days of unlimited showbiz sherbert, celebrity shagging and Spanish sunshine had arrived. Freddie Mercury was one of the first of many stars to notice.

'Freddie celebrated his birthday here with 900 guests,' explains Pike. 'We had thousands of bottles of champagne, balloons everywhere, camp fan dancers with live birds in Renaissance hairdos, four different bands and a 20-strong Flamenco troupe. Needless to say, everyone was completely out of their heads on cocaine and Ecstasy, and there were lots of gay goings on. I had this sundial in the courtyard with this metal arm on it, for example. One of the guys got a champagne cork, twisted it on to the metal dial and started fucking himself up the arse with it. Everyone applauded.'

And even when there was no party on per se, Pike could still amuse himself with the antics of his guests. Orgies in the swimming pool were commonplace, and it was considered unusual for any couple to spend a whole night with each other in their hotel bedroom.

'Things were pretty wild for a while,' concedes the Antipodean bedder of more than 1,000 women. 'After dinner it was the done thing to ask for another plate, turn it upside down and chop out lines of charlie. Then everybody fucked each other, if they hadn't already done it. Once, this wealthy German banker insisted I went down to this extension we were building on a hotel suite, and told me to "help myself" to anything I found there. He'd chained his wife, crucifix-fashion to some scaffolding. She was blindfolded, moaning and gagging for it. I did her, obviously. Pikes Hotel has always been about service.'

This new wave of Euro party-goers on the island fuelled an insatiable demand for night-time entertainment, and it was around this period that the majority of the clubs we have come to know and love were first constructed. For the most part, they were funded by Spanish millionaires with hands in political pies and good relationships with the four types of local police. Blind eyes were turned, wheels oiled, wallets filled and pills popped as the local economy boomed. People who didn't sing to the Spanish tune found themselves encased in concrete in the foundations of newly constructed hotels. Allegedly.

Then, in 1988, came the British invasion. Acid house exploded, and the Union Jack was unfurled on the salt plains of Salinas, the streets of San An, the dancefloor of Ku and the terrace at Space. A new brand of Brit-fuelled hedonism invaded Ibiza... and if you're reading this book, you probably don't need me to tell you too much about it. Except to say that it was, and still is, a lot of fun for many.

But what of true decadence? What of the heritage of the Phoenicians, Pikes, and the Romans? Does anyone still carry the metaphorical baton for perverts?

Absolutely. This is Ibiza, after all, and if it's 'relaxed sophistication' in the late 1990s you want, just head for the infamous Manumission Motel (above) outside San Antonio. This former workers' brothel is now a pleasure palace hosted by Claire and Mike Manumission for house-music glitterati and their guests. Here you will find the world's top DJs, Elle Macpherson, Shaun Ryder, Ian Brown, Kate Moss and Gerard Depardieu... more celebs, in other words, than you could shake a vibrator at. All come to drink, indulge and be entertained by the 'pleasure pussies', a bevy of genitally tattooed pole-dancing lovelies with a taste for the exotic. Unsurprisingly, the motel has also gained a reputation for corrupting the innocent, last year's infamous brouhaha involving Derek Dhalarge and Radio One's Lisa I'Anson – who failed to turn up for her own live broadcast – springs to mind.

Of course, if you tire of the VIP-only motel, there is still the Manumission club night itself to check out, an event as close to the true spirit of Ibizan decadence as you can get in a licensed club open to the general public in the late 20th century. Here, drowned in a Mediterranean of madness at around 3 am, a naked Mike pleasures his wife in front of 1,000 gurning package holidaymakers in one of the most talked-about PR stunts on the island. Arguably, at £25 a head, he's probably screwing the punters as hard as he is Claire – Ibiza's orgiastic ancients would certainly have yawned in boredom – but at least he's keeping up a tradition that stretches back centuries.

Sure, it's a long way from the ancient civilisation of the Phoenicians to Manumission's floorshow. But the links with the past grow stronger with every culture who pursue pleasure on the White Island. With each bare breast, buttock and beer, Ibiza's heritage of liberal hedonism becomes yet more unwavering, unquestionable, and – paradoxically – unoriginal.

Just like we said, there really is nothing new under the Ibizan sun.

△ **Dino Penge, clubber:** 'My only recollection is of being so desperate to go to Space that I jumped on to the back of a dustcart with two girls I'd never met before. By this stage I believed my dancing technique to be so bloody good that I decided there was no point in stopping. The two girls started dancing with me all the way, until one of them fell out of the dustcart on to the motorway. My high was only saved by the fact that she got up and started dancing on the road. At which point I pulled her up and decided it wasn't such a great idea and that I should calm down. To be fair, I can't remember anything about Space except that I left one hour before my flight was leaving for home.'

◁ **Tony Pike, owner of Pikes Hotel, on the filming of Wham's 'Club Tropicana' in his swimming pool:** 'Everybody thought it was made in the Caribbean, but it was here at Pike's. That was me serving George Michael cocktails in the video. George ended up directing it because the producer-director left all the camera gear at the airport and was fired. Andrew Ridgeley and Shirley were here as well. The three of them all stayed in the same room. I thought that was a bit strange. Anyway, at the end of the stay, I charged for two rooms, which is what they booked, but Ridgeley did a runner. He made a pile of money after that and I thought he might pay me back. But he never did, and he never apologised. Bastard.'

'Hotel Babylon', *Muzik* magazine, July 1998

Mark Spoon, Jam & Spoon: 'You boys seen a sack of coke anywhere? I'm in the mood.

'Missing In Action', *Muzik* magazine, September 1998

The legendary Pikes Hotel

View of Ibiza Old Town from El Divino

DJ Derek Dahlarge, missing in Ibiza in 1998, on corrupting Lisa I'Anson:
'The last time I saw her she was in my bedroom mumbling that she should have been on a flight two hours previously. She was completely out of her nut. I didn't think anything of it until I saw The Sun two days later. But then, a lot of people got spiked that night. It got really darkside towards the end. I lost the plot completely like Lisa. Total darkside. Total horror.'

'Missing In Action', *Muzik* magazine, October 1998

1993 the Ibiza anthems

1 LONDON X-PRESS   X-Press 2 (Junior Boy's Own)
2 DREAM LOVER (David Morales Remix) Mariah Carey (Sony)
3 PLASTIC DREAMS (Ferrari/R&S)
4 MOVING ON UP M People (Deconstruction)
5 MUZIK X-PRESS X-Press 2 (Junior Boy's Own)
6 THE NERVOUS TRACK Nuyorican Soul (Nervous)
7 OPEN UP Leftfield & Lydon (Hard Hands)
8 PACKET OF PEACE Lionrock (Deconstruction)
9 POSITIVE EDUCATION Slam (Soma)
10 DE NERO Disco Evangelists (Positiva)

compiled by Pippi – Pacha resident

Sunset on Beniras Beach

Brazilio, owner of Ku, on his yacht outside Ibiza Old Town

Cafe Del Mar

1994 the Ibiza anthems

1 GET YOUR HANDS OFF MY MAN Junior Vasquez (Tribal)

2 BEAUTIFUL PEOPLE Barbara Tucker (Strictly Rhythm)

3 LOVE & HAPPINESS Riverocean (Strictly Rhythm)

4 BOTTOM HEAVY Danny Tenaglia (Tribal)

5 FOLLOW ME Jam & Spoon (R&S)

6 CONGO The Boss (Strictly Rhythm)

7 NEW YORK EXPRESS Hardheads (Strictly Rhythm)

8 TURN ME ON Praxis Featuring Kathy Brown (Cutting Records)

9 YOUR LOVING ARMS Billie Ray Martin (Elektra)

10 FIESTA FATAL B-Tribe (East West)

compiled by Pippi – Pacha resident

Ibiza Old Town

▽ **Danny Whittle, ex-tour manager for Ministry of Sound:** 'I live for the scene and to be able to work in something you love is everybody's dream. The most difficult thing for me running such an operation in Ibiza is being able to strike the balance between taking the professional approach when needed but also finding the time to party with everybody else. My priority is to make sure everybody else has a good time – when that happens, there are no worries about what I'm getting up to! I've worked in Ibiza for four summers and I still love the island so much. It's so cosmopolitan. I love the fact that you can go drinking in the West End or go to Ibiza town and drink with Claudia Schiffer, the Sultan of Brunei or Demi Moore. And the two never overlap which means people stay in their areas, so you can choose your own environment to suit your mood.'

Sa Trincha

Emma, Ibiza worker, on the Ibiza bug: 'You can lose sight of reality here. The last time I went home, I couldn't talk to anyone for ages. I lost it. If you spend a long time in this place, it changes you way beyond recognition. My mum probably won't let me get through the door when I go back. That's why I'll be flying straight to Goa. Ever been there? I've heard it's wicked...'

'Wish You Were Here', *Muzik* magazine, October 1996

Caroline, worker, from Loughton: 'Tall Paul came back to our flat once. No, we didn't sleep with him, but there are some girls who will. Like the girl at the Manumission party who shoved a bottle of champagne up her crotch and popped the cork into the crowd. She must have been a professional entertainer. In a way, that's the trouble with Ibiza. Nothing shocks you in the end.'

'Wish You Were Here', *Muzik* magazine, October 1996

Space tattoo, San Antonio

Star Bar, 10am

▽ **Kyra Owen, clubber:** 'I just loved everything about it. Everybody was so down to earth, apart from the old-school people who kept complaining that things aren't what they used to be. I love the fact that you can just go off on your own with people you've never met before and stay up for days. I went back a year after I worked out there for Cream and I had an absolute ball.'

Kyra Owen (right) with Cream's Jim King and Gill Nightingale

Drummer at Beniras

DJ Phat Phil Cooper, Cream resident, on the cost of Ibiza: 'If you're thinking of coming to Ibiza on a budget, then fuck off. It's impossible to come over here with all this totty, booze and drugs and not spend money.'

Tony Pike on Grace Jones: 'Grace was incredible. She wanted me to fuck her within five minutes of going on stage at Ku. She always wanted it. They'd be calling her to go on stage, and she'd be saying, "Give it to me!" I did the best I could, but I couldn't keep up with her.'

'Hotel Babylon', *Muzik* magazine, July 1998

Sister Bliss from Faithless on Ibiza: 'Ibiza is the juiciest thing since Sasha's underwear! I love Ibiza because it's warm and all the clubs have cushions so you can collapse in a corner and nobody bothers you. Plus the mellow music at Cafe Del Mar is really something else. I got drunk there with Sasha once, and then we hooked up with Brandon Block and the rest is obviously history...'

Renaissance

Ibiza Old Town

1995 the Ibiza anthems

1 I LOVE YOU BABY The Original (O.R.E.)

2 HIDEAWAY De'Lacy (Deconstruction)

3 DON'T YOU WANT ME Felix (Deconstruction)

4 HIGHER STATE OF CONSCIOUSNESS Josh Wink (Manifesto)

5 THE BOMB The Bucketheads (Henry Street)

6 WEEKEND Todd Terry Project (Warlock)

7 GIVE ME LUV Alcatraz (Yoshitoshi)

8 SPACE COWBOY (DAVID MORALES REMIX) Jamiroquai (Sony)

9 I AM READY Size 9 (Ovum)

10 BOULEVARD 1-3 Saint Germain (F Communications)

compiled by Pippi – Pacha resident

Amnesia

Pacha terrace

Derek Dahlarge on going missing in Ibiza: 'I came here eight weeks ago, and I'm not going back yet. Why should I? The best part of my life here is getting up in the morning and deciding if I can be bothered going to the beach. That and the fair share of headboard rattling I've done. Unadulterated debauchery! Caning it! Shagging birds! Love it! Almost as much as meeting my all-time hero Diego Maradona, in fact. We went on a bender in Space. He was surrounded by an entourage of hookers and bodyguards, frighteningly out of his head. He stood on a table out of his nuts drumming on champagne ice buckets. Then he showed his footballing skills with an orange on the dancefloor. The whole place went wild, clapping and whooping.'

'Missing In Action', *Muzik* magazine, November 1998

Muzik Magazine on the Radio One invasion of Ibiza: 'You'd have thought it would be the dance DJs who abandoned their trollies when Radio One staged a weekend in Ibiza. But no, it was the daytime jocks who succumbed to Baleario [Ibiza flu – symptoms are looking ill, feeling worse and, in acute cases, completely disappearing]. Zoe Ball vomited in some bushes minutes before going on air for the breakfast show. Zero hours sleep and a night at Amnesia with Norman Cook were blamed. Then Chris Moyles revisited his lunch the next day, after entertaining Radio One prizewinners on the station's chartered yacht. But Lisa I'Anson left the rest looking like chronic lightweights. Preferring a big night out at Manumission, she failed to turn up for her Sunday afternoon show. Reports that she's joined Derek Dahlarge in the Ibiza loon squad were soundly denied by Radio One.'

'Radio One DJs Run Amok In Ibiza', *Muzik* magazine, October 1998

9am: Carl Cox with the Cream & Muzik posse at a villa in the middle of nowhere

CHICKEN AND CHIPS

HAMBURGER, CHIPS AND SALAD

BREAKFAST

9am: the New Star – infamous for all-day after-hour activities

chapter six

Ibiza
the rebirth

By Rob Da Bank

Pushca & Trade at Privilege

'THE BEST LAID PLANS OF MICE AND MEN OFTEN GO ASTRAY,' NOTED NAPOLEON ON HIS return from Moscow in 1798. Two hundred years later in 1998 many returning from Ibiza would have agreed with the Frenchman. Where 'plans' were made to spend at least seven hours a night in bed we spent two, where we vowed to only visit three extortionate clubs we did seven and where we promised ourselves to only spend £400 we in fact increased our overdraft by £1,000. The only plan that made it through most holidays was who was the 'best laid'?

Like a drug habit, once the White Island gets its sun-kissed talons into you there's no escape. A week, fortnight or a month earlier Ibizan 'virgins' were wondering what the fuss was all about. As they sadly climbed aboard the plane for the trip home, the new initiates were wondering why they had to go and how could they beg, borrow or steal the airfare to get back out there?

In 1988 this unique feeling affected a paltry 100 English holidaymakers, a few of them clubbers like Trevor Fung and Paul Oakenfold. Ten years later in 1998, that number was closer to 1,000,000. That's 10,000 times more clubbers amassed in a decade, and unlike other popular holiday destinations like Disneyland, Goa or Skegness, the numbers haven't fluctuated, they've just kept rising. A first visit in 1998, the busiest year yet for Ibiza, would have revealed why.

Famed for putting up with marauding travellers since the year dot, Ibiza is used to being treated like a 24-hour service station, but if the Ibicencos thought 1997 had been an

Trade

invasion of their privacy, 1998 was the apocalypse. Until you've actually been there you can't understand the reality of an island that exists like a huge playground for grown-up kids who can cavort and stay up forever. Ibiza gets a grip on you. In 1998, more clubbers than ever tasted the Balearic bounty that Johnny Walker and Nicky Holloway had glimpsed a decade before.

The tabloid press, most parents and sour-faced miserablists all saw Ibiza in 1998 as an island full of scantily-clad women and 'shirts off' men, out of their heads on beer, drugs, sunstroke and too much sex with strangers. That's exactly what it was, but so much more too. There was the girl on stage in front of 10,000 people squirting milk from her undercarriage, drug-crazed club promoters stealing an articulated lorry, entire nudist beaches shaking their bronzed bits in a formation dance to 'Gym Tonic', and Zoe Ball chucking up in a bush minutes before going live on Radio One, something Lisa I'Anson couldn't even manage as she was still tripping the light fantastic with the Pied Piper of self abuse, Derek Dahlarge.

The Brits took a fair bit of stick in 1998 for all this tomfoolery. The Spanish press misquoted the UK having a good time as 'the British don't know how to drink'. Perhaps they were genuinely fooled by the fact the English like to have a good time when they drink and don't sit staring at the sunset listening to Rachmaninov and pondering the facts of life. Indeed, the British have only just managed to pick up the basic idea that it's liberating not to have to stop drinking at 11 pm, but instead start. Admittedly, the plethora of Union Jacks, curry sauce and Ralph Lauren shirts in San Antonio must have put the wind up the authorities, but when they make parts of Ibiza look like a microcosm of Blackpool, what do they expect? Whole avenues of bars and restaurants may look suitably rustic and Spanish at first glance, but give them another look and you'll realise they're just gentrified fish and chip shops, you can't get a Spanish menu for love nor money and everything comes with chips.

Andy Koski from the Avant Garde travel agency organises custom-made clubbers' holidays for Manumission, another new trend. 'Ibiza is still the hedonistic capital of the world,' boasts Andy. 'Ibiza in 1998 was the maddest holiday season this side of a 24-hour bender with Dennis Hopper and a sackful of pharmaceuticals.'

He means the other side, of course, but wherever you stand on this, Ibiza in 1998 was about having fun. Another man to mistake having fun for something more sinister was Michael Birkett, at the time the vice-consul to Ibiza, who called UK clubbers 'animals' shortly after resigning. Not so, Michael, it's called enjoying life. To be fair to its critics, Ibiza at times in 1998 could have passed off as a massive experiment entitled 'A study into narcotic psychosis under conditions of extreme sleep deprivation'. Everyone was driving a Mitsubushi, whether it was the four-wheel moving variety or the substance that coursed around your veins making people dance like electrified baboons to Stardust... or both at the same time.

Space

Emma, Clockwork Orange flyerer, and Captain Birdseye

Manumission resident Derek Dahlarge was so impressed with the amount of 'headboard rattling' he managed in 1998 he stayed for the whole year, DJ Rocky 'thought it was so good I went three times', and Kris Needs was last spotted limping about crutchless on a broken leg after his first four days in Ibiza ever turned into one long trip. The excuse – 'well, it's the World Cup'. The scorching sun of 1998 passed unnoticed to many who spent sweaty hours twitching in hotel beds desperate to sleep before the next assault.

It would be wrong to pretend everyone who went to Ibiza ate pies all day and did so many pills a night they glowed in the dark. 1998 also saw the older Ibiza crowd retreat to the island's sacred and quieter spots. Ibiza Town, the North Coast and the hills were the stomping ground of Ibiza veterans, hippies and thirtysomethings who wanted to be able to enjoy the nightlife but stay in an area where people actually slept at some point.

Talking of nightlife, the clubs were obviously once more the sole reason for much of this mayhem. More clubbers than ever, less promoters than 1997 after some spectacular failures, and a virtual end to violent 'flyer wars' meant the field was open. All the superclubs seemed to draw capacity crowds from the day of the opening parties until the chill set in, but it was Manumission taking over the cavernous Privilege club every Monday that hit the headlines with their 8,000-strong crowds staring aghast at live sex shows, backed up with healthy rumours of sex, drugs and rock 'n' roll antics back at their Pink Pussy Motel. Miss Moneypennys alone seemed to maintain the glamorous edge on Tuesdays at El Divino with their pre-parties at Mambo resembling more of a fashion show than a clubbers' get-together. Surprise successes came in the form of cheeky outfits like Carwash mixing up Sister Sledge with Sub Sub at Es Paradis, although veteran Ibiza DJ Rocky believes many

Ralph Lawson (left) from Basics at Privilege

Backstage with the El Divino dancers

KM5 bar

Bar M

of the best parties happened away from the hype at nights like Made In Italy: 'There was just a little pocket of English like the old days. I was hard pressed to find someone who didn't speak English elsewhere, so we went there.'

Total lunatics could jump into the massive pool at Sundance before emerging to dry off in the sun gooning about to DJs like Sash, Alex P. and Brandon Block, the latter only too keen on the massive influx of Brits: 'It doesn't matter how busy it is, it's just a great place and the atmosphere is amazing.'

The hardcore (just about everyone on the island) still standing after a night out will admit that 1998 will again be remembered for the marathon Space sets during Sunday daytimes. Carl Cox's and Sven Vath's sets proved memorable, the latter even the more incredible when you take into consideration its 14-hour duration. Outside, clubbers went ballistic under the mesh roof of Space listening to the low-flying planes roaring overhead. Basics promoter Dave Beer reckons, 'It didn't get any better than Space on a Sunday afternoon. Ever.'

Ex-Cream promoter Darren Hughes agrees, 'The atmosphere at Space was electric this year. It was a melting pot of everything that's good about Ibiza, half indoors and half outdoors. The fact that it was on a Sunday meant that it was a daytime club rather than an after club, so it had less of a narcissistic vibe to it.'

And narcissism it was in 1998... as ever. Forget combats, trainers or techno. Even less underground music than usual was played in 1998, enforcing the unspoken rule of Ibiza that head nodding music or techno just don't seem to fit the bill. Happy music was in abundance.

Even the sunset in 1998 was a fiercely contested race. Should I go to watch it down at the birthplace of the sunset, the Cafe Del Mar, where the man responsible for the

. Manumission Motel`

Tony Pike on Ibiza in 1998: 'We're not a drug hotel these days. You'll probably find who you're looking for at that Manumission brothel. They're not as classy as Pike's down there, I hear, so wear your sidearms! Actually, that Mike Manumission broke his arm here not so long ago. Went to hit some bloke, who dodged and he hit the wall. Came here for a bit of peace with his wife Claire, as well!'

1996 the Ibiza anthems

1 MAKE THE WORLD GO ROUND (Deep Dish remix) Sandy B (Champion)
2 PROFESSIONAL WIDOW (ARMAND VAN HELDEN REMIX) Tori Amos (WEA)
3 SEVEN DAYS AND ONE WEEK BBE (Triangle)
4 ULTRA FLAVA Heller & Farley (Junior Boy's Own)
5 KEEP PUSHIN' Boris Dlugosh (Positiva)
6 BORN SLIPPY Underworld (Junior Boy's Own)
7 SUGAR IS SWEETER (ARMAND VAN HELDEN REMIX) CJ Bolland (ffrr)
8 WANT LOVE Hysteric Ego (WEA)
9 INSOMNIA Faithless (Cheeky)
10 GROOVEBIRD Natural Born Grooves (Heat)

compiled by Pippi – Pacha resident

phenomenon, Jose Padilla, rarely plays any more because it's too busy? Maybe I should be next door at Cafe Mambo or Savannah where Pete Tong played sets to thousands of clubbers standing in the sea or down at Bar M or Kanya? Wherever you ended up watching it, the sunsets in 1998 were one thing that didn't worry about what shoes you had on, which club you were going to next or whether you had a VIP pass to Pacha.

Despite the dressing up, Ibiza in 1998 was still one of the only places in the world where you could find rough Essex boys wearing sarongs hugging 'poncy Southerners'. It had the only clubs where otherwise well-to-do businesswomen from the Home Counties danced topless and smiling in front of beered-up lads and where 99 per cent of people on the dancefloor were smiling. Yes there were the detractors, the people Rocky calls the 'miserable sods' for whom Ibiza was less the White Island as the Shite Island. If you didn't like listening to Morales' 'Needin' U' for the 15th night running you could always find a beach or villa party, or eat in one of the superb open-air restaurants like KM5 or Es Boldado.

During the day, 58 beaches from Playa de las Salinas to Formantera and Playa des Cavallet were invaded mostly by other Europeans as the English seemed to be mysteriously nursing ailments in bed. Any appearance of English people usually led to whole beaches laughing as the pastiest people in Europe uncovered their albino skins.

One beach where the British felt fairly safe undressing in 1998 was at Bora Bora, a beachside bar down the road from Space, run by English, but over-run by Germans and Spanish. Starting out as a place to have a drink before starting work, Bora Bora quickly became the beach bar to hang out at, pumping euro house sounds out to a thousand sun-worshippers every afternoon. As promoter Sophie McIntosh noticed, 'It was brilliant but by the end of the 1998 season we got too overcrowded with tourists. We're not a club and don't want to steal anybody's business. We started out as somewhere people went before work but next year's gonna be even worse, sorry, better!'

With such a successful year under their belts the promoters of 1998 look set for a great year in 1999, and with the announcement of God's Kitchen, Gatecrasher and Scottish club Colours setting up nights, competition will be even fiercer. 1998 seemed to have bred a good balance of club nights but God's Kitchen promoter Tyrone is convinced that 'Ibiza is still wide open, and we want to be a part of it'. Attitudes like this along with the sort of coverage Sky gave the scene in its *Ibiza Uncovered* programmes and Radio One's determination to get in on the act, guarantee there are some battles left to fight.

With British summers about as pleasant as sticking your tongue in a plug socket, it's no wonder the only worry is that Ibiza will turn into a Las Vegas for the clubbing world, with strips of clubs running across the island shaped like pyramids or space stations.

The fact of the matter is Ibiza is as likely to quieten down as Whitesnake. Whether you're a 50-year-old wandering the beaches with nothing but a leather thong for company or a 16-year-old Judge Jules fan wetting yourself at Cream, the White Island is still the world's best holiday camp. Just make sure you book early.

Manumission

Alex P (left) and Brandon Block at Mambo

Phat Phil Cooper, Cream resident: 'I've been holidaying in Ibiza for years and there's a definite magic about the island, the hairs prick up on the back of your neck when you step off the plane. The Egyptians felt it too and took stones from the island to build the pyramids. The Cream opening party last year was pretty mad because I fell out of a tree on the terrace of Amnesia. I think I'd been up there about half an hour although I'm not sure why I went up there in the first place!'

△ **Brandon Block:** 'There's nowhere like Ibiza in the whole world. It's just different, you can't put your finger on why – the clubs, the people you meet, the attitudes of the people, the smell of the place when you get off the plane, even the West End is different to anywhere else. It's magical and I've seen some amazing things there. Like what? Like the sunsets, like me naked apart from a sarong, talking to a suitcase and directing traffic in the West End. People are always going on about it getting better or worse, but all that's crap – each year a new crowd come in who are old enough to go on holiday on their own. It doesn't matter who you are or what you're wearing, you can just party 24 hours a day.'

Space at lunchtime

Ben Turner, on Space in 1998: 'The best way to experience Space? Get up at 11 am, go for a Sunday roast for £3.50 at the English pub, arrive at Space just as Darren Emerson hands over to Sven Vath who opens with a CD of new Underworld material, meet the entire Boys Own posse on the terrace and absolutely lose the plot to Jose Nunez and Hector Romero. Enter dancefloor aerobics to "Gym Tonic" from every face on the London scene (plus Phat Phil Cooper on eight Mitsubishis) and general gurning all round at Bora Bora later that night. Put simply, Space is like a circus whose animals have forgotten their tricks.'

The Bora Bora beach bar – the new found land

Pete Tong at Cafe Del Mar. 7pm

Griff at Manumission. 7am

134

△ **Nicky Holloway on Ibiza in July 1995:** 'Ibiza at its worst is still better than anywhere else. But the amount of promoters trying to earn money out there is fucking ridiculous. There won't be enough room on the island for the posters! There'll be a lot of tears. It pisses me off that all these people are jumping on the bandwagon.'

Ben Turner, on the rebirth of Ibiza: 'In the five years I've been going to Ibiza, this is the best time I've ever had on the island. The British promoters who give clubland a bad name have retreated to their Ritzy homes, the jaded clubbers have finally thrown in the towel and got married, and everybody else is having the time of their life. Go to Ibiza now and treat it as Year Zero for dance music because, let's face it, for around 30,000 new Medhead clubbers in Ibiza, that is exactly what it is.'

'Ibiza '97 – Better Than Ever', *Muzik* magazine, September 1997

Perfecto illegal party

© Raise-A-Head

Paul Oakenfold: 'If you go for two weeks to Ibiza, you don't really get to know the place. For the last three years, the north side of the island have been holding open-air parties that the English just don't know about. There's nothing better than going to a party on a beautiful beach with people from all around Europe dancing as the sun comes up. It has to be secret because the clubs don't like it and would report it to the police. It's an older crowd who don't go to the clubs any more, but still come to Ibiza because the spirit of the island is so strong. If you trace back the history of the island, it's always been a playground for foreigners. First it was the hippies, then in the early 1980s it was the European jet set. I remember Freddy Mercury had an insane party. It was an undiscovered playground with all these rich people and the hippies together. Then, of course, the Ecstacy boom hit the island and eventually it was all brought back to the UK. Then everyone started slagging off the island. Which is why Jose Padilla, Alfredo, Pippi and Cesar De Malero all slag off the English. Because, in a way, we did go there and rape and pillage the island. Mind you, the British have always done that, haven't we?'

1997 the Ibiza anthems

1 AROUND THE WORLD Daft Punk (Virgin)
2 FLY LIFE Basement Jaxx (Basement Jaxx)
3 BELO HORIZONTI The Heartists (VC)
4 SPILLER FROM RIO Laguna (Positiva)
5 RIP GROOVE Double 99 (Satellite)
6 BEACHBALL Nalin & Kane (ffrr)
7 CLOSER THAN CLOSE Rosie Gaines (Big Bang!)
8 FLAMING JUNE   BT (Perfecto)
9 MOMENT OF MY LIFE Bobby D'Ambrosio (Definity)
10 FREE Ultra Nate (AM:PM)

compiled by Pippi – Pacha resident

Emma, worker: 'I love the atmosphere and the people at Manumission. Everyone's smiling and you get these mad Spanish trannies in huge platforms. You could be there in a see-through bikini and nobody would look twice. I once dressed up as a rabbit and gave out sweets to everyone. Another time, I dressed up as Benny Hill and ended up sitting in a paddling pool for hours. You can do whatever you want in Ibiza. That's what I like best about it.'

'Wish You Were Here', *Muzik* magazine, October 1996

Rob Da Bank, journalist, on Privilege: 'Walking through Privilege is like trying to ride a unicycle down the Champs Elysées the night France won the World Cup. Chocka. With the promise of a live sex show at the end of the night most of the clubbers just stand and gaze at the shag podium for hours, which kind of takes the shine off DJs Tall Paul and Sonique. Apparently the sex show happened, but I must have been looking the other way. Honest. Mind you, you don't get many of those to the pound...'

'Slumming It In Ibiza', *Muzik* magazine, September 1998

Manumission sex show

Kris Needs, DJ and producer, on discovering Ibiza in 1998: 'I met Mike and Claire Manumission last January at a party, and we agreed to make a Manumission record for Creation's Eruption label. They were in the studio shagging, so we got close. But not that close! They invited me and my girlfriend over and gave me a residency in the back room for the first four weeks. Within an hour and a half, I was sold. It was fantastic. They took us around the island – Bora Bora, Salinas, Space – and we sank right into it. It's the best place in the world, not necessarily the clubbing, but more the ambience. I couldn't imagine walking into a club – not even at Basics – wearing a sombrero, false moustache, jockstrap and bikini anywhere else in the world. We stayed the first month at the Manumission hotel where we learnt how to pole dance. There were six Puerto Rican strippers there who taught us. My girlfriend stripped. I stripped! I got debagged on stage and ended up pole dancing, but it didn't feel like beery behaviour. All the clichés you hear about the island are true. Records you hear over there take on a new meaning – you get to appreciate cheese. I mean, who could fail to enjoy Ibiza? Wine, women and song on tap.'

Mike and Claire

1998 the Ibiza anthems

1 MUSIC SOUNDS BETTER WITH YOU Stardust (Roule, France)
2 BIG LOVE Pete Heller (J.B.O.)
3 HORNY Mousse T (Peppermint Jam)
4 IN MY LIFE Jose Nunez Featuring Octavia (Subliminal)
5 HOUSE MUSIC Eddie Amador (Yoshitoshi)
6 NEEDIN' YOU David Morales Presents The Face (Manifesto)
7 PART THREE Soul Grabber (Aquarius)
8 THE HORN SONG The Don (Strictly Rhythm)
9 GYM & TONIC Bob Sinclair (Yellow)
10 1,2,3,4 D.O.D. (Prozack)

compiled by Pippi – Pacha resident

Jean-Paul Gaultier at Manumission

Caroline, worker: 'I came to this wonderful place for the first time three years ago. And as soon as I went back to Britain, I got into a really dark depression. I was in tears for two days. It was really terrible. I missed it so much that I had to get a flight straight back here. Ibiza has always had a mysterious appeal for me. Four years ago, when I was 15, a friend's brother came over here to work and I heard all these stories about naked girls walking on the beach shouting, "Hash for cash!" I really didn't think places like this existed. When we first arrived, I thought it was mad.'

'Wish You Were Here', *Muzik* magazine, October 1996

The famous Privilege swimming pool. Manumission, 5am

Manumission before...

..the aftermath

Terry Farley on why Ibiza is better than ever: 'Speaking as a founder member of clubland's "Things ain't as good as they used to be" club, things in Ibiza started to go wrong around late summer 1989, when the orbital rave hordes started to invade the garden-like Amnesia with day-glo bodies and gangsta attitudes. Since then Ibiza has been dominated by superclubs complete with a heterosexual, white English crowd. English DJs for English clubbers, playing mainstream hits for that little bit of England in the sun. A whole generation of club kids have grown up never knowing the delights of Amnesia when it truly was a club or the Cafe Del Mar before it became just one more venue along a strip that reminds you of Magaluf. To this new generation of clubbers, Ibiza is Mambo, Manumission and Es Paradis – a club playing pumping UK house and speed garage just like at home. Meanwhile clubs like Pacha have returned to different races, ages and sexual persuasions dancing to European DJs. The same beat played with a different drum. Space's mighty Sunday session is awash with the Spaniards, Germans, the odd Twilo kid from New York and fine collection of open-minded clubbers. The best DJ I heard all week was an unknown local Spaniard in the "funky room" at Pacha, playing an irresistible mix of tacky US garage and old time disco. Ibiza has sorted itself out. For old wankers like me, Ibiza – Pacha, El Divino, Zouk, Space and Ibiza Town – has returned to its former glory. For British kids going out there for the first time, Ibiza is everything you've got at home and a lot more! Ibiza has gone back to being many things to many people. So, Ibiza 1998 – the best ever! Except for when Alfredo played in 1986...'

Paul Oakenfold on Ibiza: 'It's a lot more commercial now, but Ibiza's still got the energy and spirit of ten years ago. I wouldn't say it's not as good as it used to be. It's just as good, it's just that people are a lot more familiar with it all now. It's just as special to anyone going there for the first time now as it was for me ten years ago.'

Cream at Amnesia